Inclusive Education

Policy, Contexts and Comparative Perspectives

Edited by
Felicity Armstrong,
Derrick Armstrong and Len Barton

David Fulton Publishers
London

David Fulton Publishers Ltd
The Chiswick Centre, 414 Chiswick High Road, London W4 5TF
www.fultonpublishers.co.uk

First published in Great Britain in 2000 by David Fulton Publishers

David Fulton Publishers is a division of Granada Learning Limited, part of
Granada plc.

British Library Cataloguing in Publication Data
A catalogue record for this book is available from the British Library.

ISBN 1-85346-632-8

Typeset by Elite Typesetting Techniques, Eastleigh, Hampshire
Printed and bound in Great Britain

Contents

Contributors

Derrick Armstrong is a senior lecturer in the Department of Educational Studies at the University of Sheffield. His interests include life histories of special education and the social construction of 'learning difficulties'. His previous books include *Power and Partnership in Education* and *The Assessment of Special Educational Needs. Whose Problem?* (the latter written with David Galloway and Sally Tomlinson).

Felicity Armstrong is co-director of the MEd in Inclusive Education at the Department of Educational Studies. Her research interests include: cross-cultural analysis of policy making and difference; the politics of curriculum and pedagogy; the social construction of difference through the organisation and use of space.

Len Barton is Professor and Director of the Inclusive Education Research Centre in the Department of Educational Studies at the University of Sheffield. He is the founder and editor of the International Journal, *Disability and Society*. He is particularly interested in policy issues, cross-cultural analyses and the application of disability studies in the field of education.

Brigitte Belmont is a researcher at the Centre de Recherche sur l'Éducation Spécialisée et l'Adaptation Scolaire (CRESAS) which is part of the Institut National de Recherche Pédagogique in Paris. Her research is concerned with integration in schools of children identified as having special educational needs, especially in relation to educational practice and collaboration between mainstream schools and specialist provision. She is the author of a number of different publications and is one of the co-authors of *Enfants Handicapés à l'École: Des instituteurs parlent de leurs pratiques.*

Tony Booth is Professor at Canterbury Christchurch University College. He has a long-standing involvement in the development of theory, policy and practice concerning inclusion in education in the UK and internationally. His latest contribution is: Booth, T. and Ainscow, M. (eds) 1998 *From Them to Us. An international study of inclusion in education*, Routledge.

Jenny Corbett is a senior lecturer in Special and Inclusive Education at the University of London Institute of Education. She has worked in secondary schools and in special education before moving into further and higher education. Her major research interests are in the two areas of language and power discourses relating to special educational needs and inclusive policy and practices within the post-school sector. Recent publications include *Bad Mouthing: the language of special needs,* Falmer Press, 1996, and *Special Educational Needs in the Twentieth Century: a cultural analysis*, Cassell, 1998. Her two current research projects involve an analysis of the ideological history of inclusive education and an investigation into vocational training for young people with learning disabilities, aged between 16 to 25 years, in France and Cyprus.

Patrick McDonnell teaches in a school for deaf students in Dublin. He is a part-time lecturer in the Education Department and the Equality Studies Centre at University College Dublin. He has carried out a doctoral study of the grammar of Irish Sign Language and is currently researching ideology and practice in special education.

Bengt Persson is a lecturer at the Department of Education at Göteborg University in Sweden. He worked as a regular and special teacher in schools for 15 years. Since 1991, he has worked in the area of special educational research at Göteborg University. He has a particular interest in understanding differences between special education and ordinary education and in researching the process through which some pupils become 'pupils with special needs'.

Sheila Riddell Following her PhD on Gender and Option Choice in Two Rural Comprehensive Schools, Bristol University 1988, Sheila worked as Research Fellow in the Department of Education, University of Edinburgh, investigating the impact of the 1980 Education (Scotland) Act on children with special educational needs. She then taught and researched at Stirling University and was promoted to a Personal Chair in 1995. After a period as Dean of Arts and Social Science at Napier University, Edinburgh, she became Professor of Social Policy (Disability Studies) at Glasgow University where she is Director of the Strathclyde Centre for Disability Research. She has researched and written extensively in the areas of special educational needs/disability and gender and education.

Roger Slee is Dean of the Faculty of Education at The University of Western Australia. He holds the Chair in Teaching and Learning and is the Founding Editor of the *International Journal of Inclusive Education*. His books include: *Is There a Desk with My Name On It?*, Falmer Press, 1993; *Changing Theories and Practices of Discipline*, Falmer Press, 1995; *School Effectiveness For Whom?*, with Gaby Weiner and Sally Tomlinson, Falmer Press, 1998; and *The Inclusive School* (forthcoming), Falmer Press.

Aliette Verillon is a researcher at the Centre de Recherche sur l'Éducation Spécialisée et l'Adaptation Scolaire (CRESAS) which is part of the Institut National de Recherche Pédagogique in Paris. Her research is concerned with integration in schools of children identified as having special educational needs, especially in relation to educational practice and collaboration between mainstream schools and specialist provision. She is the author of a number of different publications and is one of the co-authors of *Enfants Handicapés à l'École: Des instituteurs parlent de leurs pratiques*.

Anastasia Vlachou-Balafouti is a Lecturer at the Department of Special Education, University of Thessalia, Greece. She is involved in national and cross-national projects in the area of special/inclusive education. She has worked and studied in the educational systems of Greece, Canada and England. She is the author of the book *Struggles for Inclusive Education*.

Linda Ware is an assistant professor at the Margaret Warner Graduate School of Education, at the University of Rochester. She teaches courses in Disability Studies and Teacher Education. Her research interests include understanding disability from the lived experiences of youth with disabilities, and that of parents of children with disabilities. She conducts research in schools as they attempt educational reform for inclusion.

Athina Zoniou-Sideris is an Associate Professor at the Department of Pre-School Education, University of Athens. She has studied Psychology and Ethnology at the University of Vienna and is involved in both research and educational projects concerning the inclusion of disabled and minority students in the general school community. She is the Greek representative of Special Education/Integration in the European Community Board.

Chapter 1

Introduction: what is this book about?

Derrick Armstrong, Felicity Armstrong and Len Barton

This book looks at 'inclusive' education in the context of policy and practice in a number of different countries, particularly in relation to children and young people of school age. At the heart of the idea of inclusive education lie serious issues concerning 'human rights', 'equal opportunities' and 'social justice'. How societies construct and respond to disabilities, gender, race and cultural differences is of fundamental importance. What discourses, what legislative framework, what policy-informed provision and what resources are allocated to challenge the social practices underpinning exclusion need close and critical analysis. The extent to which the rights, privileges and responsibilities of citizenship are extended to all members of a society is a topic of increasing national and international importance.

The papers in this book will, hopefully, contribute to stimulating further debate and dialogue over both the conceptualisation and understanding of a cross-cultural approach to inclusion and exclusion. Whilst educational policies and practices are the particular focus of examination, the fundamental interest is in the realisation of an inclusive society. This includes exploring such questions as: What does inclusivity mean? What are the barriers to its realisation? How do we overcome them?

In taking this approach it is important to recognise that inclusive education is not an end in itself. Nor ultimately is the fundamental issue that of disabled people. In educational terms it is about the value and well-being of *all* pupils. Thus, the key concern is about how, where and with what consequences do we educate *all* children and young people. This inevitably involves both a desire for, and engagement with, the issue of change (Daniels and Garner 1999, Ballard 1999, Thrupp 1999).

Inclusion, exclusion and disability are not uniform categories. These papers do not offer a coherent development of ideas which move in a linear progression towards a unitary perspective on these key factors. Each analysis has been shaped by historical, cultural, global and contextual influences. This provides both the complexity and challenge to all who venture into this particular area of research.

Part of the task is to identify points of commonality and difference both within and between the papers in order to learn about others and to re-examine our own values and priorities. A crucial aspect of this process will be the generation and exploration of questions such as: How far are our educational systems democratic? Whose voices are heard and viewed as significant in the struggle for change? Whose voices are excluded, why and with what consequences? What does it mean to listen? Do we need a new understanding of the position and role of parents and the community in relation to inclusive education? Such questions are particularly demanding when considered from a cross-cultural approach (Booth and Ainscow 1998a, Barton and Slee 1999, and Armstrong and Barton 1999a).

Contexts, opportunities and rights

It is no accident that recent debates about inclusive education have arisen in part from the insistence of disabled people that their voices be heard and taken note of in the deliberation of educational policy and practice. Thus, we have seen a demand that any consideration of the role and outcomes of education be seen not simply as a technical issue concerning the relative 'effectiveness' of different types of provision but rather as a political issue of the social inclusion of all citizens in a participatory democracy. Disabled people have taken the lead in challenging and exploding the myth of a technical discourse of 'disability' and 'needs'. This is evident in books and articles written by disabled people (e.g. Abberley 1987, Barnes 1990, Morris 1991) and also in the growth of the self-advocacy movement and the political campaigns that have emanated from within this movement.

The social conditions and discourses that reconstruct difference as disadvantage have been challenged along with the social relations of a professional practice which reinforces disabling identities through the ideology of 'care' (Abberley 1992, Barnes 1992, Oliver 1992). In relation to calls for inclusive forms of educational practice these challenges have been exciting and disturbing because they have focused upon the fundamental values and principles that underlie the education of *all* children and adults. Increasingly, the issue of 'inclusion' has come to be understood in terms of a philosophy of 'entitlement'. In rejecting the discourses of 'charity' and 'benevolence' disabled people have themselves pushed for the provision of opportunities and services based on the 'rights' of citizenship.

Yet, these alternative discourses can themselves be highly problematic, giving rise to contradictions which may lead to the reinforcement of, rather than resistance to, systems of exclusion and control. In examining how this may happen it is important to turn to the historical, social and cultural contexts within and through which social practices of inclusion and exclusion operate.

Historical, social and cultural contexts of disability

The pursuit of an inclusive society involves a very difficult and demanding struggle against those cultural, ideological and material forces which combine to generate and legitimate policies and practices of exclusion. In seeking to understand the present in order to change it, it is necessary, for example, to explore some of our images of the past and how these both inform and become incorporated into our current and future endeavours.

This form of historical awareness, whilst being an indispensable component of educational reconstruction, can be individual or collective as well as haphazard or methodical (McCulloch 1994). One significant form of this awareness is that of exposing myths, including those which grossly caricature or misrepresent what is a 'complex reality'.

The importance of a historical perspective in relation to understanding the nature of exclusionary policies and practices in a given society is crucial for several reasons. First, it will act as a timely reminder that current practices are neither natural, inevitable or unchangeable. Secondly, how key concepts are defined and applied within particular professional discourses will provide an antidote to individualised and deficit models of disability. Thus, for example, 'feebleminded', 'retarded', 'special educational needs', 'special needs', 'learning difficulties' are all examples of what Corbett (1995) calls 'Bad Mouthing'. Finally, the 'voices' of disabled people have historically been excluded from debates and decisions affecting their lives. An historical awareness will provide examples of such practices and how they have been developed, legitimated, challenged and changed.

In a discussion of the changing definitions of difference Ryan and Thomas (1980) argue that:

> The changing definitions of difference constitute the history of mentally handicapped (*sic*) people. These definitions have always been conceived of by others, never are they the expression of a group of people finding their own identity, their own history. The assertion of difference between people is seldom neutral, it almost always implies some kind of social distance or distinction. (p. 13)

Not only does this perspective problematise the ways in which difference has been perceived and thus reminds us that 'yesterday's definition becomes today's term of abuse' (Digby 1996, p. 3) but it also raises the fundamental issue of power-relations and the interconnected experiences of oppression and exclusion.

For disabled scholars such as Barnes (1996) and Oliver (1996), understanding oppression necessitates engaging a historical perspective through which on the one hand, the central value system underpinning

Western culture and, on the other hand, the complex relationship between attitudes and the economy need to be carefully examined. This, they argue, will contribute to the development of an informed understanding in which ignorance and stereotyping can be identified, challenged and removed. An historical awareness provides a basis for raising questions about definitions, policies and practices in terms of whose interests do they serve and what contributions do they make towards the development of a more just and equitable society?

Disabled people have offered some examples of how to address these concerns. Thus Campbell and Oliver (1996) explore the social and political contexts within which, over a relatively brief period of time, disabled people have gained in strength as a new social movement, against enormous odds. These include chronic underfunding, a lack of faith in the viability of the new movement by many professionals, policy makers and politicians, active opposition on the part of traditional voluntary organisations and finally, because of the general disabling environment problems of disabled people meeting, communicating and organising.

Undertaking an historical analysis is a complex task in that we cannot merely read off the present from the past. It challenges essentialist ideas and thus a unitary view of disabled people in terms of holding to a singular identity. The pursuit of an inclusive society is, as Young (1990) argues, based on a view of social justice which requires 'not the melting away of differences, but institutions that promote reproduction of, and respect for, group differences without oppression' (p. 47).

An awareness of history can provide us with significant insights into the diversity of human existence over time. History is both created and recreated by human action. As Giddens (1986) notes, this is 'the double involvement of individuals and institutions' (p. 11) in that such struggles also 'produce outcomes that they neither intend nor foresee' (p. 157). It should also remind us that Western civilisation is not superior to, nor a baseline from which to judge, all other cultures. This is particularly important with the impact of globalisation and the demands for a more comparative understanding of disability and inclusion.

Historical understanding cannot guarantee the development of a more socially just and equitable society, but through an informed awareness of past conceptions, perspectives and practices, it will hopefully enable us to ensure that the struggle for change is a continuous one (Giddens 1986). Or as Borsay (1997) notes:

> it does pose a fascinating intellectual challenge which by illuminating the historical origins of cultural identity will deepen our grasp of disability in contemporary society. (p. 144)

This must also include the issue of an inclusive society.

'Equal opportunities': legislation for empowerment or a bogus discourse?

In many respects arguments concerning the struggle for a more just and equitable society have been confused by official discourses on 'equality'. The apparently high profile which has been given to 'equal opportunities' in many European countries, both at the level of government policy and at the level of institutions over the past 25 years, has masked the real inequalities which exist between different groups in terms of access to experience, opportunity and power. This is particularly true of equal opportunities in the context of education. This is not to deny the importance of equal opportunities legislation, but it should be put in its proper context by drawing attention to the contradictions between stated policy as it is found, for instance, in legislation and policy as it is enacted (Fulcher 1989, 1999) in the varied arenas of people's daily lives. These contradictions arise out of the tension created between a public rhetoric of equal opportunities and activated government policies which in all areas of public life are deepening inequalities rather than reducing them.

Equality issues and context

A number of issues and contradictions relating to equality emerge as a background to this discussion. First, although legislation has been passed in the UK over the past 25 years relating to equality issues and gender, equal pay and race relations, this has been accompanied by a massive increase in unemployment coupled with an erosion of the benefits traditionally provided by the welfare state, which has deepened inequalities in the community drastically (Hutton 1995). During recent years moves to introduce anti-discrimination legislation in favour of disabled people have received scant attention in the media and have sometimes met with cynical and well orchestrated attempts to block them in Parliament.

It has to be remembered too that there has been no legislation passed in the UK during the same period which has upheld the rights of all children and young people to full participation in an education system based on principles of equality. While the 1988 Education Reform Act introduced a 'national curriculum' on a basis of 'entitlement' for all pupils and was heralded by some as enhancing equality in education, the Act also imposed rigid assessment arrangements and a state controlled ethnocentric curriculum which has both excluded many pupils in terms of their own knowledge and cultures, and sharpened processes of selection and ranking between pupils (Armstrong, 1998). The differences between schools in terms of resources continue to be greatly increased by processes of marketisation and selection. At the same time, some groups are experiencing increased exclusion in the education system. These exclusions take place at the level of the curriculum and organisation of schools and, quite literally, by physical exclusion from ordinary schools. There is, for example, continued evidence that some pupils, particularly black boys, are more likely to be excluded from school than other pupils (Bourne *et al.* 1994). The insidious practice of unofficial exclusions is also widespread and the hidden nature of these exclusions entails an invisibility of those pupils affected. Such 'invisibility' excludes pupils on several levels, including their exclusion from the educational and social entitlements that should be theirs (Stirling 1992). The 'New Labour' government's proposals in relation to children labelled as 'with emotional and behavioural difficulties', as outlined in the 1998 policy document *Meeting Special Educational Needs: A programme of action* (DfEE 1998), show a clear commitment to strengthening intervention in relation to provision for 'children with EBD (*sic*)' including early intervention, strengthening Pupil Referral Units and assisting 'EBD Special Schools to achieve high standards'. While there is a stated policy of reducing exclusions because of behaviour, how this will be achieved in the context of increasing selection and competition between schools, is not clear.

A further question is whether equal opportunities legislation is basically designed for people who already 'belong', in the sense that they enjoy membership of ordinary institutions, or whether it really is for everybody. In general, equal opportunities discourses leave out unemployed people, homeless people, those seeking asylum, children, prisoners, and – to a large extent – disabled people. It is hard to see how these groups are included in existing equal opportunities legislation, underlining their multiple exclusions. The prevailing 'equal opportunities' project then has only been concerned with improving opportunities for some groups within certain prescribed contexts. Such a project has done little to change the power relations in society, so any gains made can be easily removed or whittled away.

Dividing policies

Historically, equal opportunities legislation in relation to different groups and the organisations which exist to protect their rights has developed along separate pathways. This has fostered a view of equal opportunities as being relevant to different groups in different ways. In the UK, for instance, the 1976 Race Relations Act and the Commission for Racial Equality are seen as serving the interests of groups who may be discriminated against on the basis of race; the 1975 Sex Discrimination Act, the Equal Pay Acts of 1970 and 1983 and the Equal Opportunities Commission are seen as protecting the interests of girls and women. Finally, the more recent Disability Discrimination Act (1995) refers specifically to disabled people. While different groups in society have particular identities, aspirations and understandings of their rights, this separate development has made it possible for legislation to seem to address equality issues relating to some groups, while neglecting others. Yet, the particular forms which discrimination and exclusion take and the degree to which different groups are subjected to them will change and vary according to the particular social and historical contexts in which they take place. For this reason the struggle is primarily about discrimination and exclusions in general. It is only within this general perspective that discrimination as it affects different groups can be understood and confronted.

The targeting of particular groups in society for 'equal opportunities' treatment has three other effects. One is to suggest that these groups are somehow naturally different and in need of special treatment, thus contributing to an image of dependency and in need of help. A second effect is that by singling out groups on the basis of race, gender or disability for special consideration (however ineffectual such consideration has proved to be), these groups are denied ordinary status and membership in the community, thus legitimating their exclusion. A further effect is to suggest that the groups concerned are necessarily homogeneous and do not represent diverse interests and aspirations. While 'disability' has not received the same attention as 'race' and 'gender' in terms of equal opportunities legislation, those policies which *have* been adopted have been divisive within the disability community itself. Colin Barnes has argued that

> because of the divisions within the disabled population in terms of age, social class, impairments and the reluctance of many to identify with disabled organisations, the emergence of a coherent political movement is unlikely. [For Oliver] these divisions are exacerbated by successive government policies, such as tax concessions to the blind but not the deaf, mobility allowance to those unable to walk but denied to those who can, and higher pensions for those impaired at work. By adopting these strategies the state keeps in check the collective interests of the disabled population and their demands for more resources. (Barnes 1990, p. 128)

Questions of policy and the contexts in which policies are adopted, then, are central to a discussion of equal opportunities. Policies do not exist in a vacuum; they reflect underlying ideologies and assumptions in society.

> these ideologies are so deeply embedded in social consciousness generally that they become 'facts'; they are naturalised. Thus everyone knows that disability is a personal tragedy for individuals so 'afflicted'; hence ideology becomes common sense. And this common sense is reinforced both by aesthetic and existential anxiety ... These anxieties have further contributed to the exclusion of disabled people from the mainstream of social and economic life and influenced policies that

have placed disabled people in segregated establishments such as residential homes, special schools and day centres. And where policies have changed towards keeping people in the community, the ideology of personal tragedy theory has ensured that policies have been geared towards doing things to and on behalf of disabled people, rather than enabling them to do things for themselves. (Oliver 1990, pp. 80–81)

While introducing some cautious reforms relating to employment, the provision of goods and services and limited access to public transport, the Disability Discrimination Act (1995) is particularly timid in relation to young people and their rights to inclusion in ordinary schools and colleges. The requirement for schools and colleges and universities to publish annual statements concerning policy and achievements is not backed up by statutory rights to inclusion which can be legally enforced, and is little more than tokenism.

Policy making and legislation in Education has failed to bring about fundamental change in structures and practices which would transform schools and make it *illegal* to deny entry and participation on the grounds of disability or difference, and education was left out of the Disability Discrimination Act (1995). This omission marks both a failure to make connections between different aspects of people's lives, and a tacit commitment to exclusionary education policies (Barnes *et al.* 1999) based on impairment. The Disability Discrimination Act itself ...

is weak because it is based on the traditional individualistic medical view of disability: impairment is the cause of disablement rather than the way society is organised. Hence, the idea that disabled people's legitimate requests for adjustments and change are considered somehow unrealistic and unnecessary is retained ... Protection is limited because not all disabled people are covered by the Act, and employers and service providers are exempt if they can show that compliance would damage their business.

Most importantly, the Act is toothless because there is no enforcement mechanism whatsoever. This means that disabled individuals must challenge unfair discrimination themselves. (p. 90)

All these arguments strongly suggest that the only way forward in the struggle for equality for all is through a struggle against *all* forms of discrimination for *all* groups and individuals in society rather than focusing attention on groups identified on the basis of official and institutionalised categorisations.

We have witnessed and experienced the failure of government legislation to eliminate or radically reduce inequalities in society. We have recently witnessed the strengthening of legislation against immigration and asylum and the introduction of laws relating to education, health and welfare benefits which are deepening inequalities in many countries in the European Union. We can entertain few illusions about the permanence or power of equal opportunities legislation or about the authenticity of public discourses relating to equality. So, while it is important to present a united front in the struggle for equality (and this includes the strengthening of legislation) it is essential to understand the reproductive role that organisational practices play at all levels in constructing differences and in promoting inequalities based on these differences. It is such a critique that underpins recent struggles for social justice that have taken a 'human rights' rather than an equal opportunities' perspective.

The politics of 'rights'

Disabled people have increasingly been at the forefront of political struggles for social reform premised not on 'equal opportunities' but on demands for 'human rights' and social justice. They have begun to challenge the representation of disability within an 'opportunities' discourse on the grounds that it discourages a critical stance towards the social conditions underpinning the experience of disabled people. In the absence of such a critique the discourse of opportunities is disempowering in that it does little more than reconstitute earlier discourses of 'care' that themselves have been substituted for political struggle against the social disadvantage and discrimination disabled people experience on a daily basis. In consequence, alternative understandings of disability have been sought which represent its social origins and offer a basis for articulating the political character of the struggle for 'human rights' in an inclusive society (Oliver 1990).

The concept of 'human rights' is not unproblematic, however. Whilst articulated as an abstract principle it is limited in its impact, and in particular may be constrained within the bounds of an ethical critique of exclusion which offers no *strategies* for bringing about change. As an ethical critique it inadequately problematises the relations of power and control that underpin the construction of the interests of some as the 'needs' of others. The language of rights may obscure their political origin. Through their abstraction from real historical and social contexts, 'rights' may be represented as 'given' rather than as secured through a continuous struggle between contending social forces.

In the absence of a rigorous socio-political critique of 'exclusion' we are left with an ethical or a technical polemic that does nothing to challenge the social power upon which exclusion is based. Thus, the rhetoric of 'rights' can also itself obscure the social critique through which the nature and outcomes of change are contested. It is important therefore to understand demands for 'human rights' in terms of specific historically located objectives. In other words, to organise around demands that contest the embodiment of dominant social interests as the 'needs' of those who experience discrimination. This is crucially important because it moves debates on from an abstract concern with the principle of equality and focuses instead upon the conditions upon which equality can be achieved while valuing difference.

A distinction might usefully be drawn between political rights, which can only be exercised in common with others, and natural or human rights which are a reflection of self-interest. John Stuart Mill (1962), for instance, was an early proponent of a view of human rights in terms that assumed an antagonism between political authority on the one hand and the individual on the other. However, at a practical level this perspective on rights has to face the problem that, in the absence of any mechanism for ordering individual preferences, competition will occur between incoherent and often conflicting demands. One response to this incoherence is embodied in the discourse of 'welfare rights', characteristically promoted within social democracies.

Whereas liberal individualism conceives of 'rights' as always asserted in defence of private interest, 'welfare rights' are represented as legitimate claims on the state to satisfy human needs. 'Needs theory', therefore, has a central role within the 'welfare rights' discourse and has been a significant feature of the development of 'special' systems of educational provision in different parts of Europe. There is an assumption that educational needs can be accurately assessed by reference to some assumed norm. Significant deviations from the norm are identified as indicative of 'special' needs requiring the allocation of compensatory resources or alternative forms of provision (Tutt 1985). Thus 'needs' theory retains the focus upon the individual that was characteristic of classical liberal thinking. Moreover, the idea of welfare rights is based upon an understanding of the role of the state as the protector or guardian of citizens against the anarchy of private interest. Thus, social democracy can be understood as functioning on the one hand through an objective order of law to regulate competing individual interests, and on the other hand to provide a cushion of support for those whose 'needs' are marginalised or disadvantaged by the social outcomes of this competition.

By contrast with its representation within liberal and welfare theories of 'rights', the concept of 'needs' can, alternatively, be understood in the context of the power relationships which underpin it; a context that comprises both cultural and historical aspects as well as interpersonal and institutional aspects. In so far as the needs of different people and of different socially, culturally or biologically defined groups are understood as different and, in certain cases, as 'special', conditions of dependency are created. Assumptions about the qualitative nature of such differences both mask and reinforce the political and social practices by which repressive forms of power and control are exercised and legitimated. Alternatively, human needs may be understood within a framework which emphasises what they have in common, in which case it is the absence of the conditions which satisfy those needs rather than the character of needs specific to particular individuals or groups that become the focus of investigation and the target of change (Doyal and Gough 1991). However, while the state is conceptualised as a neutral regulatory body, analysis of the social practices by which marginalised social interests are reproduced as 'needs' is inhibited.

Latterly the discourse of 'welfare rights' has come in for some very determined criticism. Some of these challenges emanate from contradictions between welfare discourses and the changing political and economic character of social democracies and have been articulated politically in the liberal individualism of the 'new right'. Other challenges to this discourse have come from disabled people and their organisations whose demands for change have been premised on the principle of 'human rights'. It has been argued that the representation of disability within a humanitarian welfare discourse is one that places the disabled person in the role of victim. It is claimed that the 'victimisation' of disabled people, as in charity discourses for instance, encourages an uncritical stance towards the social conditions underpinning the experience of disabled people. Disabled people are then disempowered by the discourses of 'welfarism' and 'benevolent humanitarianism' because a model of 'care' is substituted for struggle against political and social processes of oppression. In consequence, alternative understandings of disability have been sought which represent its social origins and offer a basis for articulating the political character of the struggle for 'human rights' in an inclusive society (Oliver 1990).

Conclusion

We have argued in this chapter that where calls for 'inclusive' schools and practices are limited by a framework which appeals for 'equal opportunities', or understands the 'rights' of disabled people in universalistic rather than political terms, no serious challenge is made to the conditions under which discriminatory and exclusionary social practices operate. Demands for inclusive schooling should concern not only the 'rights' of disabled children but are also part of a wider critique of that which constitutes itself as 'normal'. In the absence of such a critique, notions of 'opportunities' and 'rights' rest upon an understanding of 'normality' that reflect the partial self-interest of dominant social groups in our society. Our own starting point is that inclusive education is inextricably linked to a political critique of social values and practices and the structures and institutions which they support. The analysis of 'value' must explicate the role of education in the production and reproduction of different values, including the 'value' invested in children and young people as commodities and the representation of this value in terms of 'special' needs. In struggling for the implementation of inclusive practice we are engaging in a political process of transformation.

Chapter 2

Inclusive education in Ireland: rhetoric and reality

Patrick McDonnell

Introduction

The distinctive political, economic and social circumstances associated with the development of national systems of education create major difficulties for making cross-national comparisons between systems even in regional, as distinct from global terms. Attempts to compare policies and practices in inclusive education are even more problematic (Mittler, Brouillette and Harris 1993, Booth and Ainscow 1998): inclusive education may not mean the same thing from country to country; even within one country there may be differences among teachers, administrators and researchers as to what constitutes inclusive education.

In their general study of schools and society in Ireland, Drudy and Lynch (1993) argue that educational policy is determined by a theoretical framework that is never explicitly articulated and, accordingly, by assumptions and values that remain 'underground'. A similar process occurs when what is presented as inclusive education is, in reality, a reformulation of traditional practices in special education (Booth and Ainscow 1998, p. 7). As a first step in reaching some common understanding about inclusive education it is necessary, firstly, to uncover the 'deep structures' of special education and, secondly, to make explicit the exclusionary and segregative practices of mainstream schooling. An analysis, therefore, at the level of underlying theoretical and conceptual frameworks appears to offer rewarding material for comparative purposes (Barnes 1996).

The clinical discourses of medicine and psychology constitute some of the most familiar landmarks in the 'deep structure' of special education. These discourses possess a number of characteristic features which have important consequences for the way that special education is defined and conducted. One important feature is the centrality given to measurements of different kinds – something that clinical procedures tend to do very well. Consequently, in special education we find a preoccupation with processes that involve identification, assessment and categorisation (Dockrell and McShane 1993, Wang, Reynolds and Walberg 1995, Kirk, Gallagher and

Anastasiow 1997). Although assessment occupies a central position in schooling in general, students 'with special educational needs' become the subjects of a uniquely rigorous and concentrated professional 'gaze' (Foucault 1979, Fulcher 1989, Allan 1996).

A second element is the manner in which clinical discourses locate the 'problem' within the individual and, as a result, mask the socio-political relationship between individuals and their environments (Hahn 1985, Abberley 1987, Oliver 1990, Swain *et al.* 1993). Sets of circumstances that, from a socio-political point of view, can be seen as experiences of discrimination and inequality are characterised by clinical discourses as individualised deficits. By defining individuals in terms of 'given' problems, educationalists are then predisposed to regard educational development as having definite limits with certain kinds of pupils and the search for solutions is focused on individual deficits rather than on inequitable social structures (Drudy and Lynch 1993, p. 59). With their accompanying notions of rehabilitation and adjustment, clinical discourses further sustain this perspective (Oliver 1990, Albrecht 1992).

Thirdly, clinical discourses operate within the domain of various professionals. This creates powerful vested interests that have been, and continue to be, intimately involved in the practice of special education and in the development of policies. Bannerman Foster (1987) points to the symbiotic relationship that exists between professionals and the state: while professionals rely on the state to legitimate their authority and, in most cases to pay their salaries, the state depends upon professionals to legitimate its activities and implement its policies. The particular interests of professionals from the fields of medicine, psychology, education and religion often bear little or no relation to the needs of pupils (Potts 1983, Dant and Gregory 1991, McDonnell 1992, Lane 1993). In terms of a power relationship between professionals and pupils, pupils are in the weakest position to ensure that their needs get priority.

Fourthly, clinical discourses not only generate asymetrical power relationships between those who assess and those who are assessed (Taylor and Laurenzi 1991, Radford 1994), they also have a transforming effect on the phenomena that they measure. Again, the theoretical basis of this process is rarely made explicit. It is assumed that professional intervention is self-evidently objective, that it is based on common sense and that it is designed for the benefit of the student. In these assumptions the transforming effects of intervention are ignored: experiences of failure, discrimination or marginalisation are transformed into charts, schedules and score-sheets (Dant and Gregory 1991, Lane 1993, Davis 1997).

Clinical discourses have exerted a powerful and pervasive influence on how certain students are defined and have shaped the way in which their education has been organised. Through these discourses, special education in its various forms is characterised as a pragmatic response to particular pedagogical and organisational difficulties that arise in relation to particular pupils in the mainstream system. These discourses define the central task in special education as that of identifying 'students with special educational needs' and then of establishing appropriate programmes. Within this framework, 'inclusive education' is constructed as a 'more acceptable' version of special education: new terminology may be introduced but the segregative, pathologising deep structures remain in place and, remaining unquestioned, the policies and practices of mainstream schooling continue to represent the 'normal'.

Several recent reports on education in Ireland have given prominence to the education of 'pupils with special needs'. For the most part, these reports contain some awareness of disability as an equality issue and indicate that there is a need for 'greater equity in education' (Ireland 1992, p. 5); that 'the needs of the individual child should be the paramount consideration' (Ireland 1993, p. 19); for 'real integration' (Coolahan 1994, p. 123); for 'full equality of access, participation and benefit' (Ireland 1995, p. 24); and 'for an equality strategy in education ... based on a set of principles which potentially form the basis of an education charter of rights' (Ireland 1996, p. 172). There are, however, serious contradictions between these expressions of concern for equality and the failure of the reports to critically examine the conceptual frameworks that have underpinned segregative and exclusionary practices in education.

In this chapter I will focus, firstly, on recent developments in policy-making and planning with regard to 'special educational needs' in the Republic of Ireland. Secondly, I will try to place these developments in the context of dominant ideologies and related practices in the education system. Thirdly, I will briefly discuss the principle of inclusive education and distinguish between it and the concept of integration. Finally, I will argue that if education is to be inclusive it must be egalitarian.

Recent developments in policy-making and planning

Since 1992 six major documents relevant to our discussion have appeared in Ireland. Five of these are reports, four of which deal with education and one with disability: *Education for a Changing World*, a Green Paper on education (Ireland 1992); *Report of the Special Education Review Committee* (Ireland 1993); *Report on the National Education Convention* (Coolahan 1994); *Charting Our Education Future*, a White Paper on Education (Ireland 1995); *A Strategy for Equality*, Report of the Commission on the Status of People with Disabilities (Ireland 1996). The sixth document is the text of a proposed Education Act (Ireland 1998).

The Green Paper represented the first stage, and the White Paper the final stage, in a process of policy development and preparation for the Education

Bill. The Report of the National Education Convention marked an intermediate stage in discussions on key issues of educational policy. While these documents do not deal with the concept of inclusive education *per se*, issues relevant to the topic appear in the context of discussions about integration and special education. Both the Green and White Papers deal with integration and special education in the context of education in general. From our point of view, however, the most important documents are firstly, the Report of the Special Education Review Committee (SERC) which deals specifically with the education of 'pupils with special needs'; secondly, the Report of the Commission on the Status of People with Disabilities which discusses and makes recommendations on education; and thirdly, the proposed Education Act which sets out to enact leglislation 'to ensure that the education system is accountable to students, their parents and the state for the education provided, respects the diversity of values, beliefs, languages and traditions in Irish society and is conducted in a spirit of partnership ...' (Ireland 1998, p. 5).

In terms of inclusive education, perhaps the most positive aspect of the Green and White Papers is shown in a willingness to see disability as an equality issue. Both documents emphasise the need for greater equality in the education system, 'especially for those who are disadvantaged socially, economically, physically or mentally' (Ireland 1992, p. 5). The SERC Report, on the other hand, does not include equality as one of its guiding principles. The bland statement: 'All children, including those with special educational needs, have a right to an appropriate education' (p. 19), is the closest the SERC Report comes to a notion of equality as an issue in special education. The most positive aspect of the SERC Report lies in its forceful arguments for the provision of adequate resourcing and support services (ch. 7) and for the establishment of formal structures 'to ensure the coordination of policy-making, planning and service delivery at national and local levels' (p. 241).

The Report of the Commission on the Status of People with Disabilities was exceptional in that, of all the reports, it made the most forthright recommendations for the development of policies of inclusive education. Altogether it made 55 recommendations about education, emphasising the notion of 'the least restrictive environment' and favouring the concept of 'appropriate education' contained in the American Individuals with Disabilities Act. In particular, the report stressed the need to incorporate principles of inclusion in the Education Act. Like the SERC Report, the Report of the Commission emphasised the importance of adequate budgetary support: 'There is no doubt that the improvements needed in order to bring about equality and full participation will require additional expenditure ... Given the very high levels of disadvantage experienced by this group ... an increase [in expenditure] is justifiable and, indeed, essential in terms of social justice' (pp. 183–4).

It is ironic that, in terms of 'charting the way forward into the next century' (Ireland 1993, p. 19), the reports that deal specifically with education, and most particularly the SERC Report, are the most seriously flawed. One major flaw has been the failure to directly involve disabled people in policy-making and planning. While the White Paper claimed that 'equality of access, participation and benefit are to be promoted for all' (Ireland 1995, p. 7) none of the reports, with the exception of the Report of the Commission on the Status of People with Disabilities, attempted to put this into practice. The education reports were singularly lacking in the notion of equal respect for persons – a 'fundamental principle of equality' (Baker and Gaden 1990, p. 2). No person with a disability was appointed to the Review Committee on Special Education; neither were there any representatives from among former pupils of the special education system. Membership of the committee was drawn almost exclusively from the teaching profession and from educational administration. The composition of the committee clearly reflected the asymmetrical power relationship between service providers and service receivers in this sector of the educational system. Consequently, the SERC Report lacks an important critical perspective.

The White Paper, which appeared two years after the publication of the SERC Report, established its own philosophical framework on principles of pluralism, equality, partnership, quality and accountability. In spite of these principles, and in spite of having had opportunities to practice inclusion (Spelman and Griffin 1994, p. 134), the report does not indicate any strategic or consultative role for people with disabilities in planning for the educational services they might receive. There is no awareness shown that this might even be an issue. The White Paper merely stated that a special task force had been set up within the Department of Education to implement the findings of the SERC Report.

The education documents reflect a clinical/pathological model of disability (see for example, Ireland 1995, pp. 24–6; Ireland 1998, section 2). Accordingly, activities such as identification, assessment and categorisation are considered to be of central importance. At various stages in the pupil's school career the functions of medical, paramedical and psychological personnel are described and highlighted (see Ireland 1993, pp. 27–45). The SERC Report, for example, identifies important roles for midwives, paediatricians, nurses, family doctors, social workers, visiting teachers and especially psychologists during the pre-school years. It recommends that 'Health Boards should continue to have responsibility for ensuring the delivery and coordination of assessment, advisory and support services for pre-school children with disabilities ...' (p. 29). At primary and post-primary level, the report proposes that 'an expanded School Psychological Service ... should be established on a countrywide basis without delay' (p. 32). It recommends continuation of assessment services which fall largely under the control of the health authorities (p. 40) and that '[c]lose links should be maintained between the School Psychological Service, the School Health Service and clinic-based assessment services in each area' (p. 32).

Perhaps the most definitive evidence of a clinical/pathological model of disability appears in the proposed Education Act. The Act, by its uncritical acceptance of such a perspective, has ignored a great deal of current research in the field. It defines disability as 'the total or partial loss of a person's bodily or mental functions ... or ... the presence in the body of organisms causing, or likely to cause, chronic disease or illness ... or ... the malfunction, malformation or disfigurement of a part of a person's body ... or ... a condition or malfunction which results in a person learning differently ... or a condition, illness or disease which affects a person's thought processes ... or which results in disturbed behaviour' (Ireland 1998, section 2).

The SERC Report, the White Paper and the text of the Education Act do not communicate any awareness of the problems of interpreting disability as a clinical issue or of defining it as an inherent characteristic of the individual (Bannerman Foster 1987, Barton 1988, 1996). The documents take for granted that activities such as identification, assessment and categorisation are neutral and assume that the involvement of medical, paramedical and psychological personnel in defining, identifying and measuring impairment is unproblematic. Pupils are defined in terms of disabling attributes which can be identified and measured. They are 'those whose disabilities and/or circumstances prevent or hinder them from benefiting adequately from the education which is normally provided for pupils of the same age' (Ireland 1993, p. 18); in the words of the proposed Act, individuals 'have a ... disability' (Ireland 1998, section 2).

The documents convey no awareness of current critiques of clinical/pathological perspectives on disability, of studies carried out by disabled people themselves, or of the problematic nature of a great deal of research in the field (Rioux and Bach 1994, Shakespeare, Atkinson and French 1993). Omissions of this kind reveal a very limited understanding of disability, of relationships between disability and society, of patterns of response to difference, and of the role of vested interests in education. There is the implication that educational failure or difficulties experienced by pupils are attributable to characteristics of the pupils themselves and that patterns of low attainment stem from the nature of the impairment (Drudy and Lynch 1993, p. 63).

The manner in which the reports deal with educational provision for deaf children clearly illustrates this clinical/pathological perspective. The SERC Report defines deaf pupils only in terms of deficient hearing (pp. 104–110). There is no acknowledgement of at least 25 years of international research on deaf communities and on sign languages which indicate that deaf people are members of a linguistic and cultural minority. The Education Act proposes 'provision for students learning through Irish sign language (*sic*) or other sign language, including interpreter services' among the support services it describes (Ireland 1998, section 2). In doing so, the Act implicitly defines Irish Sign Language as a matter of technical support of the same kind as 'guidance and counselling', 'equipment', 'speech therapy', 'transport', 'library' or 'school maintenance' (section 2). Interestingly, while the Act provides an administrative context for teaching through Irish (section 31), it did not do so for Irish Sign Language. We can only conclude that because of its clinical/pathological perspective on deafness, the Act failed to provide for Irish Sign Language as a core linguistic and cultural issue.

Given the exclusion of people with disabilities from policy-making and planning, the acceptance of a clinical/pathological model of disability, and the absence of a social perspective, it is not surprising that the education reports propose recommendations that are largely of a technical support nature. Technical support solutions to educational problems can be briefly described as more identification, more measurement, more specialist personnel, and more training for professionals. Although the SERC Report proposed that 'the needs of the individual child should be paramount' (p. 19) and that parents' wishes 'should be taken into consideration' (p. 19), it went on to state that educational provision should be established on the basis of the 'individual pupil's assessed needs' (p. 20). Assessment procedures are, of course, determined and controlled by professionals. The Forum of People with Disabilities argued that educational provision should be based on the principle of choice rather than on the principle of assessment, a position identical to government policy as stated at the time (Coolahan 1994, p. 122). The ensuing White Paper did not endorse the view of the Forum.

In an extensive discussion on gender and equity, the Green Paper (Ireland 1992, pp. 9–10, 67–71) acknowledges the existence of gender bias in the educational system and it is instructive to compare the discussion and recommendations regarding gender with those regarding disability. At the level of rights, the argument for gender equity begins with the constitutional and human rights of women as individuals. No attempt is made to invoke the rights of parents of women to give substance to this argument. However, the rights of pupils with disabilities are almost always perceived in terms of the rights of parents. It appears to be difficult for policy-makers to envisage children with disabilities as having rights as separate and independent individuals; there is no vision of what the pupil is to become – as adult, as worker, as citizen.

The Green Paper goes on to emphasise the need for schools to be alert to the influence of the hidden curriculum in reinforcing stereotypes and to ensure that the achievement and contribution of women are highlighted in the curriculum. It notes the absence of women from positions of authority and power in the education system and stresses the need for appropriate role models if girls and young women 'are to develop themselves to their full potential' (p. 70). The document then outlines a detailed programme to promote gender equity in education. There was an obvious need to conduct a similar analysis in relation to disability. In particular, there was a need to address disability in terms proposed by disability organisations to the effect that 'disability is the result of disabling political and social processes which treat a functional impairment as a reason to disadvantage or marginalise individuals' (Cooney 1995, p. 249). The education reports failed to provide such an analysis.

The Report of the Commission on the Status of People with Disabilities comes closest to defining disability as a form of discrimination. It states:

> People with disabilities are angry, and their justifiable anger was evident in submissions to the Commission and at listening meetings which the Commission held throughout the country over the past two years. The picture that emerged was one of a society which excludes people with disabilities from almost every aspect of economic, social, political and cultural life ... They want, and are entitled to, equality and full participation as citizens. (p. 5)

The report goes on to take equality as its key principle; it argues for programmes of affirmative action and positive discrimination to address the past inequalities experienced by people with disabilities (p. 12).

However, the Commissions report is clearly ambivalent in its definition of disability. Initially, the report acknowledges that traditional definitions of disability have been challenged and that disability is now recognised as a social issue rather than as a medical problem stemming from some personal impairment (p.8). In the subsequent general discussion and recommendations, however, the report frequently refers to disability as if it were an individual impairment. A second weakness in relation to education is the apparent assumption that an active promotion of inclusive policies is enough; the report fails to address, as equally important, the exclusionary aspects of mainstream schooling.

In summary then, the reports have expressed varying degrees of awareness of disability as an equality issue in education. They have failed, however, to carry out two necessary and fundamental tasks that flow from this standpoint – failures that apply in particular to the education reports. They have not investigated the conceptual basis of special education and they have not addressed the reality of current ideology and practice in the mainstream education system. The failure to address existing segregative practices in mainstream education, the pervasiveness of pathologising views of the individual, and the absence of any concrete proposals to promote equality in relation to disability, forces us to doubt the seriousness of expressions of concern for 'greater equity', 'real integration' and 'equality of access, participation and benefit' for disabled pupils.

Ideology and practice in the Irish education system

The assumptions and perspectives that were discussed in the last section are very much the products of dominant ideologies in educational discourse in Ireland. Drudy and Lynch (1993) in their study of schools and society in Ireland identify two ideologies that are particularly relevant. Firstly, official reports and documents and educational research are dominated by a consensual understanding of the social order. A perspective of this kind fails to detect the role of underlying structural relations of power and wealth in generating inequalities; conflicting interests related to class, gender, race or disability are not seen as shaping influences on the educational system. Variation in educational participation and attainment is explained largely in terms of individual differences while the social and cultural functions of schools are not recognised as being significant factors in the production and maintenance of inequality in society.

An essentialist view of the individual constitutes a second pervasive ideology in Irish educational discourse (Drudy and Lynch 1993). In essentialist ideology, individuals are assumed to possess a quantifiable and relatively fixed amount of 'ability' or 'intelligence' which predetermines their educational needs. Thus, responsibility for success or failure in education is attributed to some personal deficit or impairment and, as a result, the search for solutions to educational problems focuses on the individual rather than on the wider social and cultural framework within which education is practised. As we have seen, the same essentialist perspective underpins the clinical/pathological definition of disability which prevails in the SERC Report and other documents.

In spite of a huge financial investment in education since the 1960s, there has been little reduction in social class differences in educational outcomes (Breen *et al.* 1990, pp. 130–34). While absolute rates of participation and attainment for all social classes have increased, relative inequalities between them have also increased (Clancy 1995, p. 484). The main beneficiaries of the expanded opportunities in education have been the middle and upper middle classes. Inequalities persist at several stages of the educational process. Class related patterns of school intake are particularly evident at second level (Drudy and Lynch 1993, pp. 144–5); the great majority of pupils who leave school early, with minimum or no qualifications, are from manual working class backgrounds and the proportion of pupils who remain in second level education decreases as one moves from the upper to the lower socio-economic groups (Breen 1986, p. 11); inequalities in participation rates are most obvious at the point of entry to third level education with the greatest inequalities existing in the most prestigious sectors (Clancy 1988).

Segregative practices within schools reinforce social and economic inequalities. At second level about 75 per cent of schools practice some form of ability grouping – streaming, banding and/or setting; 40 per cent have relatively rigid streaming with rigid subject distinction and little choice, leading to restricted availability of subjects (Hannan and Boyle 1987, pp. 103–5, Lynch 1989, p. 80ff.). Ability grouping has had a polarising effect on pupil attainments and attitudes: it has reduced levels of attainment, fostered poorer self-esteem and encouraged anti-school behaviour among pupils placed in lower streams (CMRS 1989, Drudy and Lynch 1993, ch.12).

At primary level there has been little direct research on ability grouping. One study, however, has shown that primary teachers group by ability on the basis of reading and maths (Carr 1988). Allocation to groups was made on the basis of teachers' judgements rather than through tests and, once established, the groups tended to remain static. Another study showed that children were very aware of differences in teacher expectations and these differences affected the children's self-esteem and self-image (Devine 1991).

Structures and practices which reproduce inequalities in mainstream schooling have the most serious consequences for the development of inclusive education. The SERC Report makes the general point that '[m]ore post-primary schools will need to adapt in order to accommodate better to students with less serious learning difficulties and to those with disabilities' (pp. 23–4). But beyond that, neither the SERC nor the other reports have much to say about the pervasive inequalities and segregative practices in the mainstream education system nor about the implications of these for inclusive education.

Obviously, all of these official documents are important. The policies and plans outlined in them are intended to provide a framework for future development. In relation to inclusive education, however, the documents articulate and maintain a perspective, a tone and a practice that continues to marginalise pupils 'with special needs': they locate the problem in the individual, look for solutions through identification and assessment and through technical supports geared towards 'adjusting' the pupil. As I have already pointed out, the documents do express some concern for equality in education but if this concern is to be more than rhetoric, education must be inclusive – in policy-making and planning, in participation and outcomes.

Principles of inclusive education

In a general understanding of the term, inclusive education draws on several different perspectives. At its most basic, inclusive education stands in direct contrast to the practice of segregated special schooling. It incorporates ideas which already have had an important influence on the debate about integration – ideas such as equality of opportunity and comprehensive schooling. In particular, inclusive education offers a way of dealing with the negative connotations of 'normalisation', a principle which has been a major force for change in the social services (Whitehead 1992, p. 55) and which has had a particularly important role in the critique of segregated special schooling. However, there are some difficulties associated with the use of the term 'normal' in education.

Firstly, there is the problem of how 'normal' is understood or determined in society. There is the assumption, for example, that what happens in mainstream schooling is 'normal' and therefore unproblematic. Secondly, there is the assumption that the 'normal' is a given rather than a social product (Davis 1997). Such assumptions overlook the fact that interpretations of what is to count as 'normal' can be imposed by relatively more powerful social groups. A good example can be seen in the educational experiences of deaf pupils. From the late 1950s, schools for deaf children in Ireland adopted what has been called an oralist policy. This meant that spoken language was literally imposed on pupils as the normal form of language in the schools; sign language was prohibited as a deviant mode of communication (McDonnell and Saunders 1993, Saunders 1997). What was imposed as normal was of course not normal from the point of view of deaf pupils nor of the deaf community.

Problems of a similar kind arise in relation to integration policies. Although integration has functioned as a powerful alternative to segregated schooling it is usually discussed as if it were a one-way process (see for example, Ireland 1993). As a result, integration is no longer a neutral term. In integration discourse, the expectation is that pupils moving from the special education sector will 'be able to cope', will 'fit in'. There is no similar expectation of mainstream schools. The inequalities that already exist in mainstream schooling have not become a central part of the debate on integration. It remains to be seen whether the new programmes being introduced at second level (Ireland 1998, pp. 51–3) will create more inclusive mainstream schools or whether they will merely reformulate existing segregative practices.

The principle of inclusive education offers a perspective that overcomes some of these difficulties. Inclusive education does not presuppose the existence of a normal group and an abnormal group nor that the latter might need to be integrated into the former. Rather, it represents a challenge to the stereotype of the normal. It recognises that education must be inclusive for pupils who have been marginalised by segregation or by labelling; it also recognises that only by becoming more inclusive can mainstream schools become more normal. Inclusive education implies a negotiated process: pupils attending mainstream schools need to be integrated as much as pupils attending special schools or classes, and the benefits are mutual.

The idea of inclusion is also closely linked to the principle of comprehensive education. This principle implies that the pupil intake of a school should reflect the composition of the community in terms of its social, cultural, religious and intellectual diversity (Booth and Swann 1987). It implies the delivery of a curriculum that recognises and values diversity and difference and that organises learning in a way that respects the multiple and varied abilities of pupils. But perhaps the most crucial element in inclusive education is the principle of equality.

Inclusive education as an egalitarian objective

Egalitarianism is best understood as incorporating a number of distinct principles of equality (Baker 1987). Of fundamental importance is the principle of equal respect for persons (Baker and Gaden 1990). Equal respect 'calls for the development of a genuine ethos of mutual respect and understanding in a single status society' (Baker and Gaden 1990, p. 2); in such a society the abilities and achievements of all citizens is appreciated. In practical terms, equal respect would mean genuine consultation with disabled people and appropriate representation on bodies responsible for policy-making and planning in education. It would mean the recognition of people with disabilities themselves as primary sources of information about disability and especially about the particular needs and difficulties experienced by them in the education system. If we wish to promote equal respect, school-going children must have opportunities to exercise these attitudes. Equal respect will not be promoted if schools engage in exclusive practices. Pupils 'cannot learn properly to participate without actually participating ... neither ... can appropriate attitudes be developed as abstractions, for exercise later on or elsewhere' (Gaden 1992, p. 2).

Another important principle is that of equal opportunity. Equality of opportunity, expressed in terms of the distribution of access and resources, has formed a central plank in the argument for integration. Inclusive education, however, involves issues of oppression and discrimination as well as issues of distribution. The pathologising discourses in special schooling and the exclusionary discourses in mainstream schooling make it clear that egalitarian principles are about more than the regulation of competition for social advancement in an unequal society. Since people have different needs and abilities, 'egalitarian equal opportunity would call for them to be treated differently, but not necessarily in a way which directs more resources to the more able' (Baker and Gaden 1990, pp. 4–5). As Young (1990) argues, social structures and institutional contexts influence the nature of distribution.

The Equality Studies Centre at University College Dublin (1994) proposes four criteria necessary for the achievement of equal status in relation to disability:

1. Equality in formal rights and opportunities
2. Equality in participation
3. Equality in outcomes
4. Equality of condition.

It is outside the scope of this chapter to explore in detail the implications of these criteria for inclusive education. However, it is possible to provide some examples of how each criterion is relevant to the development of inclusive education policies. Equality in formal rights and opportunities requires that there are no legal or quasi-legal barriers to any person's entry into the education system. Direct discrimination such as that contained in Rule 155(4)(a) of the Rules for National Schools, which establishes formal guidelines for admission to teacher training colleges in Ireland, would have to be prohibited:

> Before a candidate is admitted to a Training College the medical officer of the College must certify that he is of sound and healthy constitution and free from any physical disability or mental defect likely to impair his usefulness as a teacher; the medical certificate shall include such details as the Minister may require.

Under current legislation, there are also a number of ways in which indirect discrimination can be practised. The use of written entry tests to select or allocate pupils indirectly discriminates, for example, against those who use Braille, who have writing difficulties, or whose first language is a sign language. Equal status legislation is necessary to prohibit direct and indirect discrimination in education against pupils with disabilities and there is a corresponding need for a sanctioning system for educational institutions as well as for a monitoring body with statutory powers to enforce sanctions (Cooney 1995).

With regard to equality of participation there is a requirement to provide for basic material needs – for example, an accessible physical environment, an accessible curriculum as well as appropriate accommodation for extracurricular activities. According to this criterion, education institutions at first, second and third levels, are required to develop and publish an active policy to promote disability equality, and to record progress in implementing this policy. Administrative bodies in education would be expected to promote disability representation in their membership and there would also be a requirement to educate administrators, teachers and the student body about disability issues.

The third criterion, equality of outcomes, addresses the degree of success that pupils experience in the course of their participation in the educational system. International experience shows that the realisation of equal outcomes for different social groups is not easily achieved. Disabled people have experienced considerable discrimination in the past and, as a result, are under-represented in and excluded from many sectors in the educational system. Any serious attempt to deal with these inequalities would have to involve programmes of 'affirmative action' or 'preferential treatment'.

The criterion of 'equality of condition' represents the most radical challenge to existing policies and is concerned with the structural sources of inequality in society. It addresses those differences of status, wealth and power which reproduce class and gender related inequalities in education. Equality of condition expresses the notion of an inclusive society; it applies to all the major institutions since 'having equality of condition in other institutions is a pre-requisite for having equality of condition in education' (Equality Studies Centre 1994, p. 18). Furthermore, in education, equality of condition requires that both the formal curriculum and the hidden curriculum take account of, and fully recognise, the diverse nature of human society and the multiple forms of human abilities (Gardner 1985).

Conclusion

Predominant assumptions and practices in the Irish educational system have the most serious implications for inclusive education. There are serious contradictions between these assumptions and practices and the concern for equality expressed in recent reports on education. Although there is some awareness of existing inequalities, the reports make no attempt to address these inequalities in any fundamental way. Therefore we are forced to conclude that the concern for equality expressed in these documents is not a serious concern.

The disability movement has been excluded from meaningful participation in policy-making and planning in education. People with disabilities have had no direct represention on relevant committees and have had no strategic role at this level; professionals remain the gatekeepers of the service. The fact of the matter is that in Ireland it is very difficult for social and cultural groups who experience discrimination to achieve just and serious responses to their circumstances. Progressive social legislation, for example, often follows upon a directive from the European Community or is wrung from governments by way of the courts. It is hard to imagine an initiative being brought from the level of rhetoric into reality without some sort of external compulsion.

Of particular concern is the lack of consideration in official documents of a social model of disability. There is no apparent awareness of research by disabled people and others which has challenged clinical/pathological perspectives. Inclusive education stands in opposition to a clinical/pathological model of disability because it represents a challenge to the stereotype of the normal and it is based on the notion of disability as representing a difference, not a deficit.

Among the most positive developments in Ireland is an increasingly activist disability movement and a growing awareness that disability is an integral aspect of the debate about equality in society (Forum of People with

Disabilities 1993, Irish Deaf Society 1993, The Combat Poverty Agency, the Forum of People with Disabilities and the National Rehabilitation Board 1994). The disability movement has emphasised that disability is part of a wider and more fundamental issue of economic and social inequality; it offers an alternative to individualised and deficit models of people; it is setting its own agendas, defining its own needs, demanding real choices and opportunities. There is a growing awareness too, that in relation to disability, discrimination and exclusion are more than consequences of negative attitudes; they are products of organisational structures and institutional practices. Education is an important barometer of change in those structures and practices.

Chapter 3

Greek policy practices in the area of special/inclusive education

Anastasia Vlachou-Balafouti and Athina Zoniou-Sideris

Overview

Special education in Greece has not evolved (at least chronologically) along lines similar to those in other industrialised countries, even though the dominant policies have been highly influenced by policies and practices of other Western countries. In this paper the issue of 'special education' will be approached from two interdependent angles. Firstly, emphasis will be laid on the relevant legislation because an analysis of the existing legislation – or lack of it – reveals the political and social orientation of governmental measures on issues such as the education of children with 'special educational needs'. Secondly, the most prevailing policy practices in the area of 'special education' will be presented in an attempt to show the complexity and contradictions surrounding this area.

Introduction

Two years ago, one of the authors of this chapter approached an ordinary preschool teacher to introduce her to an inclusion project. The teacher was asked whether she would be willing to participate in this project provided there were a number of changes so as to create a suitable environment for the inclusion of a disabled child. Among these changes were the reduction of the pupil–teacher ratio and the support of a special teacher. The response was: 'I prefer to teach two classes together instead of teaching less ordinary children plus a disabled child with the help of a special teacher.'

While this can rightly be characterised as an overt expression of prejudice and discrimination, at the same time, it would be very simplistic, if not dangerous, to criticise the teacher's response in isolation from the wider context within which such responses are created. Such an approach would mean to deny the historical, traditional, political, cultural and economic factors surrounding the issue of special education in Greece. As Barton (1995) maintains:

any adequate explanation of disability must entail the deconstruction of historical, political, cultural and economic factors. These combine in various ways to provide the context against which our engagement takes place. (p. 2)

The analysis of policy practices surrounding disability and education enables us to understand the complexity of the issues involved when we endeavour to approach the ways in which societies construct, interpret and respond to what has been largely called 'special needs'. In addition this can be the beginning of a process whereby, in a context of 'cross-cultural studies' developing themes related to special/inclusive education can be analysed and a sharing of ideas and concerns can begin. I refer to a context of 'cross-cultural studies' rather than 'comparative studies' because I see this chapter as a single country case study which does not actually make any comparisons. Cross-cultural studies consist of descriptions and analyses of sets of countries with the purpose of either drawing some general conclusions based on the descriptions or to assist in the process of finding solutions for common problems among different countries (see Pijl *et al.* 1997). While there is a tendency to explore commonalities and differences between different educational systems and/or to 'copy' the experiences and practices of other countries deemed worthy of being introduced in one's own system, it would be futile to base the analysis solely on such purposes.

This study does not focus attention on the extent to which problems are common across countries or on the existence of general solutions. In fact its first concern is not comparative: however, a number of things do emerge which invite comparison (see Armstrong 1999). They are concerned with issues relating to the socio-political mechanisms by which the 'special' are socially constructed – nationally and/or internationally – and excluded from the normal education system.

A major theme of studies concerned with national (and/or local) policy practices of different countries is the extensive amount of change which is still to be made within and across societies for reducing discrimination and exclusion. As Shapiro (1981) states, disability is inevitably about exclusion. The meaning of 'special needs' is a matter of understanding the legitimised practices that underpin special needs as a phenomenon. The insights offered in an analysis of a particular national case study, while not comparative as such, can contribute in the more global quest to the understanding of the nature of the educational enterprises within which weaker social groups continue to experience exclusion. There are claims that in such studies there is considerable scope for subjective interpretation as the researcher determines the facts to be described and the conclusions to be drawn and by doing so she or he creates a particular aspect of the 'case'. There is a major dilemma related to the selection of events, policies and practices that are going to be analysed, especially when a national case study refers to an international readership which has little or no experience of the historical, cultural and political dimensions of particular countries. The principles or criteria by which a writer selects some processes but rejects others, can never, in my view, be satisfactorily justified. At the same time, however, the writer cannot be isolated from the situation under study especially when the nature and the complexity of the topic is such that it demands a context-inclusive analysis. It is this ongoing political struggle around giving meaning to actions, setting objectives and trying to interpret and understand processes that helps me to realise that:

> to keep our options secret, to conceal them in the cobwebs of techniques, or to disguise them by claiming neutrality (and/or objectivity) does not constitute neutrality ... It's naïve to consider our role as abstract in a matrix of neutral (and/or objective) methods and techniques for action that doesn't take place in a neutral society. (Freire 1985, p. 39)

In the light of the above this chapter will explore some of the policy practices involved in the construction of special education. Policy is considered as a form of practice while practices are simultaneously theoretical, moral and political (see Fulcher 1989).

Setting the perspective

In Greece, according to the official documents, the underlying political philosophies surrounding special education and/or integration are based on 'the principles of equality of opportunity in education, the idea of social inter-acceptance of disabled and non-disabled children and the promotion of educational and social mainstreaming practices and policies for children with special needs' (*Information Bulletin of Special Education* 1991, Bardis 1994). In addition, according to Article 16 of the 1975 Constitution:

> Education is the basic mission of the state, aiming at the moral, spiritual, professional and physical education of the Greeks ... and their fulfillment as free and responsible citizens ... All Greeks have the right to a free education at all levels in state school. The state shall support distinguished students and those deserving of assistance or special care, according to their abilities (as cited in the *Information Bulletin of Special Education*, Ministry of Education, 1994).

Although within the Greek Constitution there is a recognition of the right of all children to have access to free education, a number of issues indicate that there is a resurgent need for reconsideration if the laudable rhetoric is to

become reality. Some of these issues, emerging in the following discussion, pose serious questions about the nature and extent of democratisation of the Greek education system.

A critical analysis of existing legislation can serve as the starting point for exploring to what extent successive governments have had the political will to promote and support the creation of inclusive education. While we do recognise that legislation is not in itself sufficient to meet the vision of a barrier-free society, it can have a significant impact on the process of overcoming disabling conditions. In addition, the analysis of existing legislation shows the extent to which the law has been unable to protect the rights of disabled people, while at the same time, translating the rights discourse into a discourse of needs with the underlying paradoxical assumption that the introduction of 'needs' as a basis for educational and welfare state practices will reduce inequalities.

The legislative framework of special education

During the first half of the twentieth century, the majority of disabled children, perceived as the social stigma of their families, were (and some still are) isolated within asylums, segregated private institutions or behind the closed doors of their homes. Disability was, and still is, accompanied by feelings of guilt and embarrassment. It is an occurrence in life that is better hidden since disabled children tend to be targets of curiosity, pity and often fear (Salpistis 1987). Such discriminatory attitudes originate from and reflect the social racism inherent within institutionalised practices and policies which historically have violated even the basic human rights of disabled citizens (Papaioannou 1984, Bitzarakis 1989, Tsiakalos 1989, Stasinos 1991).

The education of disabled children was solely dependent on private and/or religious charitable initiatives. The dominance of the private sector over this area as well as the great numbers of illiterate disabled people, was a result and reflection of the non-existing legislative framework to ensure the right of disabled children to be educated. As Kouroublis (1994) indicates, this was 'a period in which the State had not realised its responsibilities resulting from the United Nations declarations with regards to human rights' (p. 70, translation ours). Private initiatives were solely based on the 'politics of institutionalisation' connected with an extensive sector of residential or total institutions in the sense of Goffman's asylums (Goffman 1968, Kitsaras 1994). The notion of education was limited in the scope and nature of the work done at sheltered workshops whenever such workshops existed in the institutions.

Even though within such initiatives there were motives of humanitarianism, accounts of the social origins of segregation must go further in order to seek other interests as well (see Tomlinson 1982). Such moves to isolate disabled children and adults were based on accounts of their possible danger to society (Stasinos 1991). Such accounts very largely contributed to the stigma still attached to notions of disability. Furthermore, such moves were connected to the broader socio-political and historical context of Greek society at that time. Institutionalisation was a political control mechanism which aimed at the 'moral correction' of the 'immoral' and 'deviant' youngsters. These 'troublesome youngsters' originating mainly from the poverty-stricken lower classes (Stasinos 1991, Kouroublis 1994), were the social products of a country facing serious socio-political and economic problems associated predominantly with a number of successive, devastating wars. Given the above context, a strong discourse on defectology in the child and psychopathology was developed which strengthened, and was strengthened by, the increased powers attributed to the medical profession. The strong influence of the defectology discourse on issues of deviance has been until now one of the main models of resistance towards the creation of more inclusive educational communities. At the same time the repercussions of the philanthropic ethic according to which disabled people were defined as objects of pity, dependent and eternal children, while non-disabled people had the moral duty to protect and give for the 'needy', are still felt today in popular media programmes which aim at raising funds for rehabilitation centres.

The above practices are partly the result of the institutionalised policies of the welfare state in which the discourse of needs thrives. But as Fulcher (1989) so powerfully reminds us, in a discourse about needs the question of 'Who defines these needs?' is a key political question. The reality of the welfare state includes a number of institutionalised factors – professionals are part of this reality – that determine definitions of 'needs' by affecting (and/or being affected by) the quality and quantity of services provided to people. In addition, 'despite the apparent humanitarianism implicit in the notion of needs, the evidence suggests that where resource allocation has been made in welfare states on the basis of "need", groups so defined become marginal members of society' (Fulcher 1989, p. 262). This reality can be transferred in an educational context as well, since the first Act passed by the Government in 1951 (904/51) was heavily based on the notion of needs, especially the needs of blind children. The Act referred to the education of blind children and the policy of cost-of-living allowance. But it was not until 15 years later that the effects of the 1951 Act were, partially, realised. The Government of the Liberal Union, by passing the Educational Act of 1964, went to some lengths to modernise and democratise the ordinary educational system. For instance, it made education free of charge and for the first time, with a nomothetic clause, referred to the education of blind children in ordinary schools. In practice, the legislation was not fully supported by the creation of the adequate infrastructure and resources that would help its implementation (Kouroublis 1994).

Still, up to 1980 both policies and practices concerning special education were strongly connected with initiatives undertaken by the private institutionalisation sector. According to Kalatzis (1977):

> The main characteristic of these special institutions, especially the private ones, was the enrolment of as many students as possible. The two or three well known institutions had special schools with 200 and 300 students; a phenomenon that reminds us of 'the settlements' or the 'villages of disadvantaged children' that existed in other countries quite long ago. The lack of schools and teaching classes for disabled children was enormous ... As far as the teaching personnel was concerned the picture was frustrating ... The vast majority of the teachers (91 per cent), who taught at special schools, did not have any specialised qualifications ... (p. 37, in G. M. 1983, translation ours)

This was the situation that the architects of the 1981 Act concerning special education had to face. The 1981 Act introduced by the Conservative political party has been considered as the first political action to establish the legislative dimension of special education. The Act recognised, for the first time, the responsibility of the state for disabled children's education. It established the creation of the Directorate of Special Education within the Ministry of Education, which is an administrative agency directly connected with issues relevant to the education of disabled children. Further, it introduced the creation of state special schools and special classes in ordinary schools as well as the creation of new professional disciplines such as special teachers, child psychologists, speech therapists and also strengthened the importance of specialisation. Finally, it introduced the creation of the so called Special Advisers.

Even though the 1981 Act intended, to some extent, to make popular the issue of special education, a critical analysis of its basic ideology indicates that it has perpetuated and even strengthened the discourse of segregation and defectology on issues of disability. As Fragou (1989) maintains:

> Forty years after [the introduction of the 1944 Act in Britain] the Greek Government copies models and totally ignores the social issues raised in other countries. It ignores the social issues which have developed under pressures from the people who have been affected in the first place by such policies. (p. 62, translation ours)

The 1981 Act was not incorporated within any of the main Educational Acts. It referred not to the education of disabled children but 'to those who deviate from the norm'. Thus, it focused on defining in a dogmatic way the term 'deviant people', and categorised children according to their impairment and/or perceived disabilities. Its language was insulting, while some of its propositions lacked any educational rationality. For instance, the document relating to the 1981 Act claimed that graduates from Departments such as the Department of Home Economics, and Baby-Preschool Nursing were able to teach in special schools due to a shortage of special educators. As a disabled writer wonders in his analysis of the Act:

> What is the relation between a special educator and a graduate of Home-Economics? ... unless they consider that both jobs qualify someone to feed, to clean the house and to take care of the children; then yes, maybe they are related. (G. M. 1983, p. 35, translation ours)

Such irrationalities in terms of policy have been indicative of the way popular discourses viewed the nature of education when disabled people were concerned. In terms of practice, they devalued the concept of being a special teacher which in turn was an extension of the historical devaluation of disabled children who were perceived as inferior and not worthy of being taught.

While the 1981 Act and its ideology has influenced practices regarding the education of disabled children, it was not implemented because in the same year the Conservative Party suffered a defeat by the Socialist Party. Another major event in this year was the incorporation of Greece in to the European Union (EU). From 1982 onwards, the new political discourses, influenced by wider European trends, claim that the Ministry of Education is in full support of integration. The new government passed the 1985 Act concerning the 'Structure and Function of Primary and Secondary Education'. It was claimed that the orientation of the Act was to reconsider the ordinary educational system and to incorporate, for the first time, special education within the process of restructuring the broader educational framework.

In practice, both the 1981 and the 1985 Act resulted in the increased tendency of creating special schools and/or special classes within ordinary schools. For instance, while in 1983–4 there were only seven special classes, in 1992–3 there were 602 such classes. As far as special schools were concerned, while in 1978–9 there were 67 special schools, in 1992–3 there were 200 special schools. The 1985 Act introduced the notion of 'special needs' while at the same time maintained the ten 'categories of handicap' which formed the basis for the development of special schools. Special education became a popular area and a direct result of its popularity was the creation of more special schools and the enrolment of an increasing number of so called 'students with special needs'. For instance, within the period of one decade (1982–92) there was a significant increase in the enrolment of students in special schools; from 2,725 in 1982 they reached the number of 12,383 in 1992.

At the same time, complex notions such as 'integration', 'inclusion', 'equality of opportunity', became quite suddenly very popular in political discourses. These terms, according to governmental claims, had served as the basis for the introduction of the 1985 Act. While governmental claims talk about equal opportunities, the educational practices and more specific conditions indicate that there is no enabling legislation to support the views expressed. The integration discourse, instead of focusing on pedagogical practices including the political economy of schooling, organisational issues, staff development and the curriculum, focused on issues of disability. But the political and practical tactic of placing disability rather than the curriculum as the object of concern constitutes the basis of a divisive ideology that maintains exclusion. Referring to equality of opportunities and integration, while at the same time focusing on disability and its synonyms, can create a number of practical and ideological conflicts.

Ideological crossroads and educational policy practices

It seems that any attempt to understand 'what is happening' in the area of special education will result in confusion and puzzlement since special education seems to be dominated by contradictory and confusing political and practical discourses (Xeromeriti 1994). This is partly because the notions of 'special/segregated provisions' (1981 Act) and 'integration' (1985 Act) were introduced within the same decade; the first being influenced by the 1944 Act in Britain and the latter by the British Warnock Report and the American concept of the 'Least Restrictive Environment' (PL. 94-142 Act). Thus, while in other countries these complex notions were introduced within a period of more than a hundred years, within Greek society both notions were introduced almost simultaneously, generating social and practical confusion as to what equality of opportunity in special education means. Both Acts, but most importantly, the most recent Act of 1985, while introducing a specific ideology, lacked any basic specifications and programmes that would promote its implementation (Zoniou-Sideris 1996).

In addition, the confusion surrounding the area of special education has been partly the result of adopting uncritically concepts and practices that have been developed and have been criticised in other countries. Such uncritical acceptance denies the enormous economic, cultural and political diversity that is to be found among different countries, even those which are normally regarded as European. Further, it belittles the importance of the historical struggles that have taken place in other countries before and after the introduction of processes such as 'special education', 'integration' and 'inclusion'.

Currently, in Greece and according to the popular way of thinking, integration in the wider community can be achieved through attendance at special schools and more recently special classes in ordinary schools. In fact, according to the dominant discourses – including teachers' views – terms such as normalisation and socialisation are used interchangeably. In practice, this means that disabled children have to be educated in special schools and/or special classes with the assumption that in this way they [children] will acquire those characteristics that will help them to fit into society; to become as 'normal as possible'. In these terms, socialisation has been defined as normalisation.

Furthermore, the word 'integration' is used in both positive and negative ways. Statistics here can be of some help. Even though research in the area of special education is only in the early stages, it has been estimated that, within the total population of children in Greece approximately 180,000 to 250,000 children have 'special educational needs' (Nicodemos 1994, Papadopoulos 1988, Ktenidou 1990). In 1994, the Directorate of Special Education reported that only 14,136 of these children are educated in special schools or in special classes in ordinary schools, while 3,500 pupils receive special help from units run by the Ministry of Health and Social Welfare. Where are the remaining children with special educational needs? While some of them remain at home without any type of education, the vast majority attend ordinary schools. Let us offer an example here. From research concerning the education of 408 children with hearing difficulties/disabilities, in 1989, it was found that: 37.7 per cent of deaf and hearing impaired children were being educated in ordinary schools with very little or no support at all; 33.3 per cent were educated in schools or classes for deaf children, while 7.4 per cent were in other special schools together with mentally disabled children. Finally, a large proportion (21.6 per cent) of deaf children were not provided any type of education. The researcher concludes:

> The educational p'.acement of children with hearing difficulties/disabilities takes place in an arbitrary way, without any planning or valid criteria ... The most worrying element is that deaf children are educated in ordinary schools without special intervention programmes or any other support. (Lambropoulou 1994, p. 468, translation ours)

The above information becomes even more worrying if we combine it with the following significant issues. First, the vast majority of children are being educated within state educational institutions and are provided with all the required school texts free of charge. However, a careful examination of the nature and structure of the ordinary education system confirms that 'law cannot achieve substantive rationality, or goals of the kind implied by the notion of free education' (Fulcher 1989, p. 270). Parallel to the state education, a strong private tutorial network has been established which children make use of after school hours. An increased traditional mentality has emerged according to which academic success through the state education system can hardly be achieved without extra private tutorial classes. For those whose socio-economic background prevents them from attending such classes the educational competition takes place in an unjust and unequal way. It has been found that the majority of the families with children who have been defined as having special educational needs face a situation of long-term poverty (Kogidou and Padazis 1994). This is related to other findings according to which a large proportion of the so called children with special needs originate from low socio-economic classes (Zoniou-Sideris 1991).

A second significant issue is related to the physical geography of the country with its mountainous areas and its extensive coastline and hundreds of islands, widely spread over the Aegean and Ionian seas which give rise to particular problems in the care and education of disabled children. This, in conjunction with the concentration of the population in Athens, has encouraged, and has been encouraged by, a strong centralisation of services which has led to the creation of 'privileged/urban' and 'non-privileged/rural' areas. This differentiation has a significant impact on the quantity and quality of the education, health and social services provided, as governmental policies tend to show lack of social sensitivity and political commitment to respond to the needs and complexities of the latter areas (Papadopoulos 1988, Davazoglou 1994, Bardis 1994). Thus, the quality of educational response to the child is largely dependent upon the opportunities provided by the family's financial and geographical situation. This comment can be made to 'a lesser degree of educational opportunities in ... some other parts of Europe' (O'Hanlon 1995, p. 127).

Given the above conditions, the fact that the vast majority of children with special educational needs are in ordinary schools does not justify political claims of supporting integration. It rather indicates that the official definition of integration remains at the level of locational integration. But locational integration alone, in practice, means total rejection. In fact, the majority of children with educational difficulties/disabilities are educated in ordinary classes with minimal support due to lack of resources for the creation of segregated special provision. This can partially explain why there is a tendency of various agencies, and parents of disabled children, to demand the development of special schools or special classes. As Zoniou-Sideris (1993) maintains 'the existing educational policy aims ... at the establishment and the extension of special/segregated schools' (p. 21, translation ours).

There are also demands for the expansion of diagnostic centres and the development of the historically marginalised professions of educational psychologists, counsellors, and speech therapists. The area of special education has started to become a developing industry with the involvement of more professional groups which endeavour to establish and develop their interests. A common characteristic of the newly introduced professions is their strong attachment to a medical approach towards learning difficulties/disabilities. Further, the prevailing lack of specific Higher Education Departments for training special teachers has generated the feeling that there is an urgent demand for the development of specialism and the acquisition of specific skills for teaching these children (Papadopoulos 1988). Even though there is a need for raising teachers' awareness of the challenges that the education of disabled children poses; at the same time, a crucial point needs to be raised. When the training of special/support teachers is mainly based on a discourse of deficits, negatively-valued difference and professionalism, there is a danger of separating skills for teaching those who are deemed disabled from those who are deemed 'normal'. In such cases the underlying assumption has been that children with special educational needs belong to a different pedagogical category and thus cannot be taught by ordinary teachers. Such institutionalised pedagogical assumptions have been identified as perpetuating and even strengthening a divisive ideology that impinges upon efforts to create more inclusive educational apparatuses (see Tomlinson 1982, Fulcher 1989, Mousley *et al.* 1993).

School policy practices

The above divisive ideology has become the basis for the creation of almost every pedagogical practice. Of course, schools differ in how far they integrate students who are perceived as having special needs. That means that they differ in the way they try to respond to the demands that a wide variety of students pose on implementing the curriculum. From this perspective, integration practices mean successful ordinary educational practices in terms of responding to the variety of needs that a teacher encounters in her or his class. Within this context some schools tried to integrate the so called students with special needs even before the word integration was introduced into political discourses. The institutionalised factors that impinged upon teachers' efforts to create more responsive educational practices were maintained after the introduction of integration in official political documents.

This is partially a result of the fact that even though the Education Act of 1985 went a step further by approaching special education as part of ordinary education, it has failed to change the basic characteristics of the ordinary system that render it predominantly exclusive in structure and nature for both ordinary and the so called children with special educational needs. By failing to do so, children with learning difficulties/disabilities with very little or no support at all confront an educational system which:

- Has not been designed with them in mind.
- Is unable to adjust to their difference due to its rigidity.

- Imposes a latent uniformity on the curriculum, syllabuses and teaching material.
- Has a history of a strong central bureaucracy which, in turn, has been in good part responsible for producing the low efficiency of the system and its inertia despite attempts to modernisation and democratisation.
- Favours abstract academic learning, demands high intellectual abilities, advanced oral communication and written skills, reinforces a deductive way of thinking in the area of science, emphasises memorisation rather than critical thinking and experimental learning, and is based on a didactic way of teaching.
- Has created a highly selective system with a strong competitive dimension that demands teaching towards examinations, which in fact are multiple and determinative. For instance, two thirds of Lyseum graduates (senior high school) remain outside the institution of higher education because 'the inability of the economy of the country to absorb large numbers of highly educated workers has never managed entirely to satisfy the demand for higher education' (Kassiotakis and Lambrakis 1994, p. 102); and finally,
- Lacks adequate material and human resources. This seems to be a prominent characteristic of the educational system as a whole and is associated with the delayed socio-economic development of the country. Even today, Greece is struggling to emerge from a largely agrarian society to a more industrialised one.

In practice, the quality of children's education has been merely dependent on the nature and degree of teachers' commitment and goodwill. But the nature and degree of teachers' commitment is greatly influenced by the context within which they have to work (Vlachou-Balafouti in press, Vlachou 1997, Vlachou and Barton 1994). The existing prevailing context has reinforced the perception that inclusive priorities are either an additional burden or are extremely difficult to implement. Often, ignorance and prejudice are additional factors in maintaining and perpetuating exclusive structures.

Given that pedagogical structures have not changed in the direction of inclusion, there is an increasing demand for the creation of special individualised educational programmes. Most of these programmes are improvised by unsupported teachers who have not been trained in issues relating to learning difficulties/disabilities. Often these programmes are incomplete, lacking clear educational objectives and the means to be implemented. In addition, the Directorate of Special Education (Nicodemos 1994) informs us that:

Today, we create school units and other special educational programmes for the education of children with special needs. However, the scientific base of such programmes, the support of the teachers who are working in this area, the inspection, as well as, the coordination of these programmes do not take place either by the Peadagogic Institute or by the few Special Advisers ... or by any other educational organisation. Thus, many of these programmes have been underdeveloped, ignored and often their implementation has been postponed. (p. 25, translation ours)

Thus, the children whose needs are not met by the existing educational system are defined – mainly by their teachers – as children with special needs. This broad and ambiguous term has been adopted from other countries (for example Britain) within whose socio-political climate it has been used, in different contexts, often for perpetuating segregated education (see Tomlinson 1982, Fulcher 1989). This term implies that the child has to be treated, cured and even normalised. But, as Barton and Oliver (1992) claim, 'by emphasizing the pupil's failure the fundamental issue of the system's failure to meet the needs of all pupils is masked' (p. 14). Similarly, as Fragou (1989) points out:

The history of children with 'special needs' does not indicate their inability to adjust to their educational system; it rather indicates the rigidity of the educational system and its inability to adjust to their differences. (p. 63, translation ours)

In comparison with the past, one of the positive aspects of the current trends is that the integration of disabled children and adults within the wider community has started to become more visible in different arenas even though such processes are at an early stage of development. The underlying values and assumptions informing official educational policies have begun to be questioned. An increasing number of ordinary teachers have emphasised the socio-political dimension of integration and its complexity (Anagnostopoulou 1994). At the same time there is a strong tendency to focus on an individualistic tragic approach towards disability issues while educational practices are organised around a notion of disability that strengthens the creation of professionalism based on a medical perspective.

Some attempts have been made, mainly due to initiatives by teachers, to create educational activities that would promote social interactions between disabled and non-disabled children (Papaioannou 1992, Agalioti 1992). However, in practice, the majority of these initiatives are individual school attempts, which have remained at the level of locational and social mainstreaming practices. Thus, they have failed to problematise the core curriculum, deflecting attention from the need to implement the substantial changes needed for establishing inclusive priorities.

At the same time, parents of disabled children have become more aware of the existing exclusive societal structures. There is, however, a need for more coherent and collective parental groups that can act as pressure agencies in facilitating change (Papagalia-Katriou 1987). In addition, the majority of the existing parental groups, especially parents of mentally disabled children, are still under the strong influence/control of medical persuasive discourses, which emphasise a clinical approach to issues of disability.

There is still a long and difficult way to go in challenging the mythology of care upon which the politics of institutionalisation, dependence and segregation are based. Struggles have to be intensified towards the analysis of the institutionalised barriers that disabled people face in realising full participative citizenship. Collective action from groups constituted by disabled people is of great significance in this area. However, the absence of disabled people's voices is in itself striking. As Barton (1991) maintains:

> this absence ... is not because they have nothing to say, via the available mediums, but that they are explicitly prevented from speaking. This is related to the ways in which disability is defined and to the expectations and practices associated with such definitions. It is fundamentally about unequal social relations and conditions and the ways in which power is exercised in our society. (p. 6)

Conclusion

The aim of this chapter was not to reach any final conclusions but to contribute to the discussion regarding these policies and practices that impinge upon efforts to recognise the rights of disabled people and their value as equal citizens. In other words, we tried to explore these social–educational and legislative relations and conditions that impinge upon the creation of more inclusive educational communities. We, ourselves, in the effort to understand the concept of exclusion as it has been imposed by the structural and social organisation of society, are left with a series of difficulties and questions for which we have no immediate answers. Questions such as 'Where does equality of opportunity in education rest within the current educational practices?' 'How and to what extent is legislation used to promote the purposes it seeks to challenge?' 'What does "Schools for All" mean in the way this statement has been used in government pronouncements?' as well as 'What kinds of curricula and organisation do schools need to develop if they are to become truly Schools for All?' are of great importance if rhetoric is to become reality. What we have no doubt about is that disabled children and young people are still not entitled to the same kind of schooling opportunities as their able-bodied/able-minded peers. Exclusion and segregation have been built on centuries of devaluation. Most of us, including teachers and researchers, have not grown up or been immersed in a culture where inclusion and friendship with disabled people has been an ordinary and typical life occurrence. Segregation and marginalisation will not only survive but they will be further established as long as ordinary schools fail to become truly Schools for All.

Chapter 4

Sunflowers, enchantment and empires[1]: reflections on inclusive education in the United States

Linda Ware

Without a doubt, special education policy in the United States, is influenced by federal mandate dating back to the 1975 Education for All Handicapped Act (EHA), now known as Individuals With Disabilities Act (IDEA, 1990), and by The Annual Reports to Congress. The Annual Reports are benchmark documents published by the United States Department of Education which describe the progress made by each state towards the implementation of IDEA. Even a cursory glance at these documents indicates that with time, obfuscation has greatly diminished in the name of clarity, utility, and availability. In as much, it is important to point out that prior to 1997 the Regulations did not address specific outcomes for students with disabilities as much as it stressed getting students into schools and receiving services. In many ways, the 1997 Regulations added fuel to the conversation on special education and inclusion primarily because the general state accountability systems were directed to include students with disabilities.

In this chapter I will borrow from several Annual Reports to Congress (1994, 1997, 1999) which describe nationwide efforts to strengthen educational opportunities for the six million students with disabilities in America's schools. In addition, I draw from previous and ongoing research in public schools with teachers, administrators, students, and parents in Kansas, New Mexico and New York as each attempted to restructure their schools for inclusion (a more complete description of this work is available elsewhere as noted in the specific references within this text). My selection of segments of this prior research is intended to address the project for this book specifically relating to the relevance of policy on inclusion reform. Thus, it is important to begin with a definition of inclusion. In prior work I have attempted to convey the challenge of defining inclusion when virtually every professional and institutional practice of twentieth-century schooling would come under scrutiny and be deligitimitised as a consequence of inclusion (Ware 1995a). Specifically reform would challenge: placement, assessment and evaluation (for both students and teachers); the language of demarcation common to schooling practices; the goals of schooling, and life after schools for all students; and the overarching goal of how we intend to live together in a society. When translated into local, state, and national action, inclusion becomes synonomous with 'inclusive schooling' and its attendant policy areas of curriculum, student assessment, accountability, personnel development, professional training, finance, and governance (CISP 1998). Framing inclusive schooling according to these technicist constructs fails to explicitly inform understanding about schools as legitimised sites of exclusion, and thus minimises the cultural interrogation central to the project of inclusion (Ware 1996b, 1997d, 1998b, 1999a, 1999b).

I view inclusion as a social justice project that begins with understanding how exclusionary we are in schools and in society, how we are sanctioned to maintain exclusion, and how we are rewarded to remain exclusionary – all of which suggests that deconstruction would be the most useful tool for analysis. However, as a researcher in public schools, I must contend with the current notions of 'inclusive schooling' as the stepping-stone to understanding the larger project of inclusion in society. At every turn, I work as Corbett and Slee describe in Chapter 9 of this book, as a 'cultural vigilante' to expose the limitations of the technicist obsession to construct inclusion as anything less than a social justice project. The research I present here spans a decade of such efforts.

Researcher context

Over the past decade I have worked as a university-based researcher and consultant for the Kansas Board of Education (1990–7), the New Mexico Department of Education (1996–present), and currently as a school district consultant in a large urban district in the state of New York (1998 -present). Perhaps the only attribute common to these states is that local interpretation of policy and practice is, to varying degrees, borne of unique histories (individual and collective) that contribute to a range of experiences (private and public), some of which inform this research. However, commonalties across the states or even within the sites are mostly useless if the assumption is intended to suggest a 'United States context'. None such exists. My research emerges from epistemological, ontological, and methodological assumptions that preclude the presentation of simple or complete accounts. Given the demands of investing in local contexts, inside local meanings and in partnerships with local players – complexity is assumed.

Changing the context

The 19th Annual Report to Congress (1997) contains policy language in support of inclusion presented as 'the changing context of classrooms' suggesting that as general and special education reform come together these players 'increasingly influence how special education programs are defined and how students with disabilities are being educated' (I-1). Similarly, upon the release of the 20th Annual Report (March 1999), Judith E. Heuman, assistant secretary for special education and rehabilitative services, explained:

> [T]his package of regulations [is] designed to help parents, teachers, and school administrators understand the federal expectations for educating children with disabilities under the law. We have protected the basic rights of children with disabilities to a free appropriate education while ensuring that schools have the flexibility and tools necessary to offer a quality education in a safe environment. (US EDInfo, 1999)

It is important to acknowledge that although the regulations are permissive of inclusive education, they do not require inclusion. Individual states have the discretion to compel, through regulatory language, progress toward inclusion in much the same way that a school district might compel schools, and individual principals might compel their teachers to consider inclusive educational practice. Across the 16,000 school districts in the US various responses to inclusion have been reported (Lipsky and Gartner 1997), but on the whole, inclusion in the school context is neither uniformly understood, readily accepted, nor willingly acted upon.

State and local policy

States have the autonomy to create policy informed by national policy and sources they deem appropriate which must be negotiated among the Legislature, the State Board of Education, and the State Education Agency. The tensions and conflicts inherent in any one of these systems, along with the different constraints imposed on the various operational structures of each, suggest that efforts to negotiate policy would be a challenge. Adding to this is the realisation that state policy is played out within regions, cities, school districts, schools, and classrooms in unique and unpredictable ways. Complexity, contradiction and irony are 'givens'. For example, early in the 1990s, the National Association of School Boards of Education (NASBE) published a definition of inclusion which appeared in their frequently cited, *Winners All: A Call for Inclusive Schools* (1992). Language in this document was specific to the neighbourhood school placement and appropriate services in the general education classroom in an effort to end the special yet separate status of special education. States which utilised this language in their own policies would later realise that despite their best intentions, inclusion, like special education, was uncritically conceptualised as a place rather than a service. Whereas a more critical conceptualisation of inclusion as a vehicle for social justice and political action in schools and society was far from conceivability.

Generally, policy is enacted in ways that, on the surface, may align with the original intent of the law, but it can be argued that the spirit of the law remains elusive and unrealised. Ever hopeful that policy may provide important answers for the challenge of implementing inclusion, the fact remains that special education remains locked in an impermeable practice tradition rooted in reductionism. With an emphasis on fragmented 'bits-and-pieces' of understanding, reductionism stands in contrast to constructivism and has been criticised as one of the most significant challenges to understanding special education from a paradigm other than functionalism (Heshusius 1982, 1989, Poplin and Stone 1992). While once there was the belief that the field of special education would shift to holism and an interpretivist paradigm for understanding, such hopes have yet to be realised. Despite the conversations that emerged over a decade ago on mainstreaming, and those most recently on inclusion, the field of special education remains divided by traditionalist and inclusionist thought (Brantlinger 1997). For this reason, I never grow weary of citing Sarason and Doris (1982) who originally challenged the technicist approach to mainstreaming, pointing out that:

> At its root, mainstreaming is a moral issue. It raises age-old questions: How do we want to live with each other? On what basis should be given priority to one value or another? How far does the majority want to go in accommodating the needs of the minority? (pp. 54–5)

Our failure to consider these questions relative to mainstreaming has resulted in the reproduction of injustice and inequity in education despite the so called shift to inclusion. Today, it is quite common to hear educators and administrators claim, 'she's the inclusion teacher', or 'this is our inclusion class'. To my ears this signals that the rest of the faculty must be the 'exclusion teachers' who practice in 'exclusion classes.' In initial meetings with district administrators in New York, I was told that in response to the 'labelling issue' they distinguished their classes as 6:1:1 (six students, one para-professional and one teacher), or in the least restrictive setting, a 15:1 (no para-professional assistance). With that said, the administrator explained, 'we have our 6:1:1's at School 72', or 'she's the 10:1:1 teacher at School 18', or 'he's really a 6:1:1 but his mom insists we put him in a 10:1:1' (Ware 1999c).

Corbett's three tier model of inclusion described in Chapter 9 of this book is useful in analysis of this phenomenon. The first level is led by policy and notions of school effectiveness; the second, reflects structural modifications to the school environment and to the curriculum, and the third level, that of deep culture, is characterised by:

> the hidden curriculum of fundamental value systems, rituals and routines, initiations and acceptance that forms the fabric of daily life. It is at this degree of inclusion that real quality of life issues reside. This can be an intangible process whereby students are taught to see themselves as either valued or de-valued group members.

Corbett holds that the third level is the most 'satisfying type of educational inclusion' and, while I would agree, my experience in schools suggests few who attempt this level of reform are satisfied, but many are sacrificed (Ware 1999c). Despite the obvious combustibility of interrogating the system to expose its values, rituals, routines and initiations, I continue to urge districts and state education offices with whom I work to begin with the moral challenge of understanding inclusion. As a researcher, committed to the broad possibilities for inclusion, I enter knowing our efforts will teeter between satisfaction and sacrifice (as the accounts that follow reveal) but what remains as the ethical unknown is how to ready individuals and the systems in which they work for reckoning with exclusion first, so as to better understand the need for inclusion.

Kansas: the Sunflower State

The state director of special education for many of my research years in Kansas was Betty Weithers slightly under five feet tall. To those who questioned the need for special education accountability reform, Betty was famous for her 'broken record' response, 'what part of ALL don't you understand?' Her efforts focused on the inclusion of students with disabilities in the state accountability systems, predating the policy recently reported in the Twentieth Annual Report to Congress (1999). Her position was far from popular at the time, for the same reasons that states report today. That is, because standards-based reform in several states has failed to include students with disabilities, general educators have failed to feel accountable for students with disabilities (Elliot and Thurlow 1997, Roach and Raber 1997, Schnorr 1990). The policy language is now explicit in that the exclusion of students with disabilities from the general curriculum, district assessments, district accountability will no longer be tolerated.

At the time, individual districts were urged to define inclusion as they saw fit. For example, in Lawrence, the special education advisory board borrowed from a number of sources to create an informational brochure, *Inclusive Schooling Means Belonging* (1995) that was used to educate the community about inclusion while schools simultaneously explored the possibilities of inclusion (Ware 1995b, 1998a, 1999a). The brochure contrasted belonging versus not belonging and tied more explicit language from the inclusion literature to the district's mission statement. This should not imply that efforts at inclusion in Kansas were all seamless or successful. Inclusion across the state generated reactions similar to those generated nationally and internationally, where resources, personnel preparation, staffing, policy, curriculum and the need for a clear definition of inclusion (the same technicist obsessions) were key challenges.

Nonetheless, in Kansas, efforts to reform special education were coordinated across three broad areas of investigation: (1) inclusive education, primarily a special education project coordinated by the state's special education team; (2) Quality Performance Accreditation, primarily a general education project coordinated by the state's general education team; and (3) school-linked, coordinated service integration which combined social, health, and education professionals in interagency coordination of services (Sixteenth Annual Report, 1994, ch. 5). While the 1990s were characterised by notions of best practices, school effectiveness, portfolio and competency-based measurement, and conversations on the merit of high stakes testing, in short, all the incompatible elements that are viewed by practitioners as contractions in practice; the state made measurable progress toward inclusion. That is, empirical measures (numeric) indicated success with the state's stated outcomes.

In those same years, I conducted qualitative research in a variety of settings in Kansas with students, parents, teachers, administrators and superintendents who participated in the critical dialogues I utilise in my research. Together, we slowly teased out issues that contributed to a larger conversation on inclusion, although the focus remained on the local conversation. Ironically, this research (also empirical), was less easily reduced to evidence to support progress toward inclusion outcomes for the state. That is, in conversations with high school youth, we probed the unconscious techniques of surveillance practised in schools and reflected on abelist entitlement relative to social justice; in conversations with parents we puzzled over the promise of inclusion and all of its unknowns and complexities; and in conversations with teachers we struggled to acknowledge the myth of professionalism as they attempted innovative curriculum. Were these conversations to be reconstructed in a manner similar to that which I crafted for my dissertation research (Ware 1994), the exchange would provide coherence across the individual dialogues, however, each dialogue occurred in isolation. The research emerged over time, and in response to needs of the participants rather than as a consequence of a larger a priori scheme devised by this researcher[2]. It was always hoped that these dialogues would contribute to policy reform, but those actual connections remained less clear. My sense at the time was that policy acts remained more the work of a 'man behind the curtain' despite the fact that many of my colleagues at the university, may well have been 'the man'. That is, the state department and the university of Kansas maintained a good working relationship, as both were well funded by the federal government office of special education research.

However, relative to Corbett's three tier model, statewide efforts in Kansas did not progress beyond the second tier. Given the multiple players and the inability of systems to 'come clean', critical self-analysis across the system was more difficult to sustain than it was on the individual level. My outsider status as a researcher made it somewhat easier to build and maintain trust with research participants, despite the initial challenge of 'ivory tower' intrusion. By their own assessment, and despite the difficulty of engaging in self-probing dialogue to come, to come to terms with the myths played out in our schools and in society, the participants in this research reported satisfaction with the processes. That is not to say that sacrifice did not occur, but rather that the scope of this research was relatively 'safe' and less contestable because of decisions I made as a researcher to contain the work within the local context. Moreover, at the time, the full impact of inclusive education had yet to be realised. The struggle would become more contentious over time in Kansas, in much the same ways I report for New Mexico and New York.

New Mexico: the Land of Enchantment

The New Mexico State Department of Education educational policy on inclusion was among the most progressive in the 1990s. This policy declared:

> The New Mexico State Department of Education believes that all students must be educated in school environments which fully include rather than exclude them. School environments include all curricular, co-curricular and extra curricular programs and activities.
> Full inclusion means that all children must be educated in supported, heterogeneous, age-appropriate, natural, child-focused classrooms, school and community environments for the purpose of preparing them for full participation in our diverse and integrated society.

More to the point, the state challenged the current arrangement of schooling as inadequate to inclusion because it was based on a 'typical/atypical paradigm'. In explicit language the policy challenged the unquestioned practice of identifying dysfunctional students, and then through placement decisions, arranging for someone else to educate them. Further, this document added, 'the inability of children to measure up to an arbitrary and subjective idea of what is typical communicates to the child and others that the child is unable to perform and that something less is expected from that child' (1991, n.p.).

This 'cut to the chase' policy suggested a willingness to broach issues related to the hidden curriculum in schools given its specific language for educators. According to the policy, 'a teacher with a vision of full inclusion incorporates high expectations for all students, and understands that everyone learns cooperatively and that schools are both places of learning and social institutions'. By all accounts, New Mexico offered the promise that substantive issues of educational reform in general and special education could be broached. However, I soon discovered that among my colleagues in special education at the University of New Mexico, inclusion was a 'non-issue' (Anderson 1990). In his analysis, Anderson views 'meaning management' as one of several 'unobtrusive mechanisms of control' utilised to mediate the social construction of organisational rationality whereby some social phenomena are sanctioned as 'events' and others as 'non-events'. Although Anderson initially located this critique in public schools among administrators, he has since utilised a similar analysis for understanding institutions of higher education as sites of institutional violence (personal correspondence).

Within the department of special education at UNM, both state policy and the national debate on inclusion were erased by faculty with little or no attention paid to the significance of these events in their courses. Teachers in my research reported that no mention of inclusion was made in their teacher preparation programmes, or that only negative accounts were provided. One participant who earned her masters degree at the university explained, 'I left the program (special education) believing that inclusion was a bad idea – that's the way it was presented to us' (Ware 1999d). Ironically, although explicit and progressive state policy did exist in the Land of Enchantment, it had little impact on the day to day lives of teachers as they struggled to create inclusive classrooms with varying degrees of commitment from their districts. In this context, my research differed significantly from previous efforts in Kansas where the university and the state worked collaboratively to interpret, rather than ignore national efforts to promote inclusive schooling.

In my first year in New Mexico, the State Education Agency (SEA) invited the five institutions of higher education to consider a collaborative effort to evaluate the progress of inclusion across the state. UNM proposed an investigation consisting of both quantitative and qualitative components. My colleague in this research was a visiting professor in the department and likewise, a 'rabid inclusionist' (Ferguson 1995). Building on her prior research, she would investigate the relationship between instructional context, teacher behaviour, and engaged behaviour for students with severe disabilities in general education classrooms (Keefe 1999, Logan and Keefe 1997). Likewise, building on prior work informed by a Foucauldian analysis,

I interviewed students and their teachers as they described what was done to them (both students and teachers) as the subjects of the disciplinary power of special education. I attempted to make tangible that which had thus far been obscured in my own research, wondering if I too was guilty of 'romanticised' accounts of inclusion (Barton 1997, Slee 1995). That is, although the critical dialogues revealed to individual participants the inherent contradictions and ironies in schools and society, the accounts of the research tended to romanticise 'possibility' as a consequence of these realisations. And this in fact, was not always the case. With a focus on the satisfaction experienced rather than the sacrifice I likewise witnessed, my intention was to describe possibilities as a vehicle to encourage others to engage with the inclusion project. After all, who would be willing to consider inclusion if they knew the challenges involved? In retrospect, it was the tidy endings that I now trouble over – the suggestion that 'all wrapped up nicely' – when all continues in wholly new iterations of complexity.

Although the New Mexico research is continuing, several presentations were made at state education planning meetings, administrative functions such as the Quarterly Meeting of State Directors of Special Education (Ware 1997d) and state conferences (Ware and Howarth 1998). One presentation focused on the perspective of high school students was titled, 'What we've done to ourselves by doing these things to them' (a line borrowed from Foucault, cited in Philip 1985) who was utilised in this analysis of special education. The paper was introduced with a call for self reflection among the audience members given that the students' accounts of special education were so powerful and stark. The students characterised special education as they 'lived the experience' – one described it as a prison from which he could not escape unless he moved to a new school and somehow his paperwork was lost; another offered that he knew students who had successfully escaped; another described years of accepting her teacher's regulatory practices before coming to the realisation that special education was less for 'her own good' than for the good of her teacher; and another explained that he had given up trying to 'pass' among his friends, and instead employed resistance by boasting, 'I tell them I'm a SPED – everybody knows it anyway' (Ware 1998b, 1999b).

Across the state, response was generally positive to both components of this work suggesting a willingness to probe and explore the everyday acts of exclusion in schools that preclude progress towards inclusion. In all fairness, I was not in New Mexico long enough to examine the sustainability of this progressive policy and its potential for social transformation, but I remain a consultant to the state on this research. It does, however, bear mentioning that within the university's special education department, inclusion remains a non-issue despite the growing success of the dual-license[3] program now coordinated by the co-PI on this research, Liz Keefe.

Researcher reflections

With each iteration of my research, I seek to make explicit among the participants the task, as Foucault frames it, to 'know what they do ... why they do what they do ... [and] know what they do does' (Foucault, cited in Dreyfus and Rabinow 1982, p. 187). Complexity, contradiction, and irony were obvious themes throughout the research conducted in both Kansas and New Mexico. These themes played out in differing ways in each state given their distinct history and context, to ultimately inform the challenge of initiating and sustaining inclusive education in policy and practice at the time. 'At the time' bears repeating, given that indeed the current context for the implementation of inclusion is important to consider. In many ways, the past was marked by a certain naïvety as the comprehensive nature of planning for inclusion revealed its richly contextualised meaning and the complexity of reckoning with the inherent exclusionary practices and beliefs in schools came to be known. On this Barton (1997) suggests:

> Everything currently seems to be against an inclusive outcome, including the increasing marketization of educational planning and provision, the intensification of competitiveness and the increase in selection, both in terms of access and experience within schools, and a set of values which celebrate individualism thereby making the possibilities of cooperation, collaboration and difference, at an institutional and individual level, less desirable or possible.

Understanding this context demands that educational researchers engage approaches that are more explicitly political and thus, more contentious. Allan (1999, p. 124) urges that we 'transgress against imperatives, whatever the risks involved'. Her charge, informed by Foucault, describes the ethical work that each of us (students, parents, teachers, researchers, policy makers, etc.) must do on ourselves. On the whole, this is a daunting challenge, one which Allan views as 'necessarily never complete, always in process' and 'driven by an insatiable desire for more' (p. 126). In the section that follows, the research elaborates further on the premise of how to conduct research when the expectation for all is to 'know what they do ... why they do what they do ... [and] know what they do does'. Because this research has just begun, I present only a glimpse into one high school's early attempts to develop inclusive education policy.

New York: the Empire State

Similar to my research in Albuquerque, upon moving to Rochester, I was invited to join the city school district's Task Force on Inclusion because of my university affiliation which in turn led to interactions with teachers at the invitation of district administrators. Before I describe this effort, it is useful to contextualise the setting which was marked by three important influences. Hereafter, the city school district will be referred to as the District.

First, in 1981, a class action suit was filed against the District, and it is currently under a Consent Decree (1983–84) and Enforcement Order (1993–94) to create more inclusive schools[4]. As a consequence, the Inclusion Task Force was an 'oversight' committee established by the courts to include District administrators, a parent, teachers, university faculty and one of the attorneys who filed the class action suit. The committee was chaired by the Director of Special Education Instruction (hereafter, the Chair). Monthly meetings were generally well attended and the interactions were positive and supportive. Although critical issues were raised, and discussed (e.g. minority over-representation, administrative leadership, instructional opportunities), action on these issues was not the charge of the committee.

Second, demographics from the city and District are consistent with national trends reported for large urban areas where steady growth by low income families, and those whose first language is not English is increasing (Feagin 1998, Hodgkinson 1999). The local media frequently report on these figures, but the significance of their impact on school progress or urban development is rarely considered. One such account (Towler 1998), reported that in 1997, 90 per cent of students in the city schools received free or reduced lunch, a figure contrasted to 22 per cent in 1980. For every 100 students who were freshmen in the city schools in the fall of 1993, only 68 were in the 1994 sophomore class, only 46 were in the 1995 junior class and only 27 graduated in the spring of 1997. Of this number, five received a Regents diploma (discussed below), and 15 went on to college. In contrast, the neighbouring 17 suburbs in the county reported that for every 100 freshman, 95 moved to the next grade level, and 84 graduated with their class. Rates of poverty in the suburban districts vary from an average of 30 per cent for schools in the inner ring of suburbs, to less than 10 per cent in the outer rings (those further away from the city). Similar to other urban cities in the US, the suburbs emerged as a consequence of 'white flight' from urban areas dating back to the 1960s, a phenomenon Feagin (1998) describes as 'urban apartheid'.

Third, in 1998 standards driven reform in New York state prompted the New York Board or Regents to raise academic standards, phasing in more stringent graduation requirements for the class of 2000, and eliminating the lower track diploma known as the 'local diploma'. Although the new standards would impact many students, it was particularly so for students in special education, many of whom graduated with a local diploma or a modified IEP diploma. Not surprisingly, before the school year ended, a special legislative panel was called in the state's capital to consider the impact of this reform, particularly tougher diploma requirements, fourth and eighth grade achievement tests and special education changes termed, 'too-much, too soon' (*Democrat and Chronicle* 1999).

Coming to know

According to a document provided by the Chair of the Inclusion Task Force at our first meeting for the 1998–9 school year:

> Inclusion began in the 1988–89 school year when the District received approval from the State Education Department to serve students with disabilities in Blended classrooms. Inclusion continues to grow through the School Based Planning Team (SBPT) process of developing and implementing innovative models for the delivery of special education services'. (District doc., April 1998, p. 2)

This document provided a revised definition of inclusion, and description of the three models appropriate for inclusion[5], and the District's 'Inclusion Roll-Out Plan' (a four year model). According to the Chair, although some classrooms were already 'inclusive', few schools viewed themselves as 'fully inclusive'.

Early on I was invited by the District to provide 'technical' support to the District's 'mini-grant' schools, 11 targeted schools that had applied for and received mini-grants ($3–5,000) to explore inclusion (seven elementary, two middle schools, two high schools). The grants were made to schools with few strings attached although they were expected to keep informal documentation of their efforts and to present progress and setbacks at two District meetings. I focused on the two high schools, and along with the district inclusion coordinator, attended monthly meetings at Morgan and weekly meetings at Wellington. By mid-year, Morgan's monthly meetings were put 'on hold' for a variety of reasons (no 'official' account offered). Meanwhile at Wellington, initial conversations about the impossibility of planning for inclusion in a climate of tougher standards had slowly shifted to accounts of classroom successes and experimentation consistent with the District's three technicist models. The five person team included three teachers Mary, Mike, Mary Ann, and Liz, a house administrator assigned to the special education students (hereafter, the Team). The principal was designated a member, but due to Wellington's preparation to launch a prestigious International Baccalaureate programme, she attended only one meeting near the end of the school year. Wellington, with a student population of 1,100 and 120 faculty, was well regarded in the district for its focus on achievement and excellence. Students were assigned to one of three houses (Science/Technology, Academic Excellence, or Transition Tech (TT)). They graduated with a specific diploma from each house which required more credits than would otherwise be earned in the District, with the exception of TT, the house for the special education students. Upon completion of required credits those students received a local diploma or an IEP diploma.

The weekly Team meetings included the district inclusion coordinator and myself, and midway through the year, Liz began to attend. The district inclusion coordinator provided the bulk of information about the district's expectations for compliance with the decree order. As a consultant I provided information from the literature, clarified questions, raised questions, but with the exception of coordinating trips to area sites, I viewed my involvement as minimal given my lack of local historical/institutional knowledge. Despite my participation on several levels, at several schools in the district, I felt I lacked the authority to press the teachers to think in terms beyond the technicist approach underscored by the District. It came as no surprise that after four months of weekly meetings the Team decided to draft a proposal for inclusion that would focus on creating more teaming situations with workshops on teaching strategies as the vehicle to provide better services to all students. Since this proposal required the approval of SBPT (a policy making body in each school) the Team agreed to create a powerpoint presentation to demonstrate successful teaming for inclusion. Mary and Mary Ann were in highly satisfying co-teaching partnerships and Mike, with a long history of similar experiences, agreed to develop the presentation to showcase inclusion success at Wellington. For authenticity, they decided to include student testimony about their own perceptions of success in the blended classes. Although this later component paralleled my previous research with students and teachers in New Mexico, I had yet to share that work with the Team. Ironically, the Team's motivation to include the students was similar to the New Mexico teachers who hoped they would hear affirmations of success from their students. However, what the teachers in both states came to know from their students was less about academic success and more about the social injustice they experienced in schools.

Similar to the New Mexico teachers, the Team was wholly unprepared to hear the accounts offered by the students who named the everyday mechanisms which label and exclude them as TTs. In a brief exchange with the teachers prior to the presentation, Mary said, 'You know, these kids even call themselves TTs'. To which Mike, nodding in disgust, replied, 'Well, yeah, why shouldn't they, that's what we call them, isn't it?' In their interviews, the students described the everyday rituals of pre-enrolment procedures for classes in which their forms are stamped with bold lettering, SPC (special), as are their report cards, and their student identification cards. In addition to the fact that TT was housed in the basement, students also cited the exclusionary practice of receiving no textbooks which signalled to others their TT status. More importantly, the students described their reluctance to participate in the formal graduation ceremony because each house bestows their own diplomas during the ceremony. The resulting ritual for them was another public demarcation that signalled embarrassment rather than celebration.

Taking the risk

Somewhere between the time the Team came to hear what the students recounted, and to know their own unwitting complicity in these processes, they revised their presentation. The goal was to persuade the SBPT to work with them on the articulation of a philosophy for educational inclusion. Teaming and instructional strategies would be presented along with various philosophical perspectives about inclusion, in addition to excerpts from the students' exchange. As well, the Team would recommend the elimination of the TT house which they now viewed as a separate and unfair placement. On a technical level, the presentation was very well done, but as a vehicle for persuasion at SBPT, it failed. During their presentation, there was a noticeable change in body language with the SBPT audience as I noted sighs, squirming, and snickering in hushed commentary. After the presentation the Team was dismissed with the invitation to return the following month to answer any questions (consistent with SBPT protocol). Emotions ran high as the Team pushed the cart of computer equipment back to Mike's room. Mary Ann offered, 'I thought I was going to cry. I just hoped I wouldn't, I had to tell myself, don't cry.' Her comment reflected the emotional power of the presentation which captured so well what they had come to know as a Team. The others speculated about what might have provoked the disturbing response, wondering if the presentation was too long, too corny, or too honest. Although there was a tremendous sense of relief that the presentation was over, despite all their efforts there was little sense of satisfaction.

A few days later, the team repeated the presentation for the Chair of the District Inclusion Team. Unlike the SBPT, he was elated with the presentation and suggested the Team present it across the District. However, the enthusiasm ended when the principal joined the meeting, and in the few minutes remaining, declared she would not endorse the elimination of the TT house and admonished the Team for proposing this idea without informing her in advance, despite her failure to attend prior to the year's end. The silence that followed her words dissolved the enthusiasm that had previously filled the room.

When it became apparent that no one else would respond, I explained that the proposal had been a long time in the making. I recounted the diligent efforts made by the Team, their site visits, their weekly meetings, the readings, their debates, and the struggle with issues that surfaced, all of which ultimately led to the conceptualisation of their proposal. I offered that because the proposal specifically invited the SBPT to consider ideological concerns about inclusion, it was among the most progressive work underway in the District. This perspective was underscored by Mike, who insisted that Wellington would be more successful with inclusion if the faculty could first clarify their beliefs about inclusion/exclusion. On his words, the bell abruptly ended the meeting.

Living with the risk

Following the SBPT meeting the synergy among the Team markedly deteriorated. With the knowledge that no action would be taken until the June SBPT meeting, the weekly meetings were cancelled due to increasing demands common to the end of the year. Prior to the meeting the Team was presented with 47 questions from SBPT to address at the June meeting. Although most were questions of mechanics, many signalled value concerns similar to those Sarason and Doris warned must be answered about the relationship between education and society. Among these were:

> How can we insure this will not make instruction even more difficult?
> What subject area classes are really possible for inclusion?
> Who determines if the rights of regular education students are infringed upon?
> Who will change parenting styles?
> Who is responsible?
> How will students in each house be informed?
> How do special education teachers feel about this?
> How do our parents feel about this?

Upon receiving these questions the Team felt misunderstood, defeated, and insulted. They had expected some questions about the mechanics of scheduling students and teacher teams, but were quite unprepared for the challenge to the philosophy for inclusion they articulated and their own ideologies they revealed. The tone of the document was offensive and difficult to overlook, and as a consequence, the Team made little effort to disguise their 'attitude' in response.

As Corbett and Slee remind us in Chapter 9 of this book, inclusive education is a 'distinctly political, "in-your-face" activity' which will demand tremendous courage by individuals inside systems who challenge long-standing mechanisms of control. The Team found themselves doing political work they did not know was necessary as they moved closer to 'knowing why they do what they do and to knowing what they do does'. Their actions positioned them against a long history of status quo beliefs and practices in schools, routinised actions that legitimise inequality by individualising failure. Listening to the students challenged these teachers because they saw reality from their students' eyes, and because they listened, they were motivated to challenge the system. At this point, these teachers have just begun to capture the imaginations of their colleagues as plans for the upcoming year specific to planning for inclusion, are still underway. Two members of the Team have joined the SBPT team, whether their efforts will revert to technisist obsessions or progress to critical dialogues to explore the inherent exclusionary practices of schools is yet undecided.

Conclusion

These accounts show the messiness, the 'in-between-ness' as Corbett (1997) describes the process once individuals realise that inclusion is about more than the issues of special education, of schooling in general, and of reinventing systems. Particular histories and contexts were suggested as important to understanding the evolution of inclusive schooling and its relationship to inclusion in each of these three states, but no explicit themes were drawn across these sites because these particulars emerged and came to be known by both the participants and this researcher during the course of conducting this research. Again, as I stated earlier in this chapter, my own understanding of inclusion is one which subsumes inclusive education as part of the larger goal of social justice. When I work in schools, I point this out with the realisation that many will remain locked within an understanding framed by technicist obsessions and policy language that dilutes the cultural analysis. For many, the system rewards preservation of the status quo (read exclusion), nonetheless, my research seeks to centre understanding on cultural awareness across race, ethnicity, gender, class, and disability. The project is not specific then to special educaton. As Bernstein (1996) explained, there are certain individuals in schools who are routinely denied enhancement, inclusion and participation, but to assume that those students are exclusively those in special education programmes, wholly misses the point of inclusion. Many have argued that examination of special education as a consequence of inclusion can lead to greater understanding of exclusion inherent in general education. Each of the states reported here began to make those very connections, but their lessons may not have appeared to them at the time in the language of 'lessons learned'. I avoid framing my research in this manner, although others with whom I have been in partnership conform to this model of research reporting. On the whole, this work is best characterised as a project of deconstruction of the values, beliefs, and interests of a few individuals who made the effort to understand inclusion inside their schools and against or within the lives they lead.

Clearly, the issue of informing or dismantling the system remains. The impact of policy on this process is questionable in that policy does not show us what we cannot see. By that I mean that until policy shifts to wider frameworks for analysis and capitalises on previously unexplored methodologies – policy will not show us, it will merely tell us through geometric equations (Ware 1995b). Currently, policy implementation relies on patriarchal assumptions which are interpreted and managed within systems whose goal is oftentimes mere 'symbolic policy compliance' (Marshall 1997, p. 7). In her calls for interpretive and narrative policy analysis, Marshall suggests that 'cost benefit analyses give way to the microanalytical, sociolinguistic, ethnographic ... to include methodological approaches utilising life histories; discourse analysis, deconstruction of policy texts, journals that reveal self-identity negotiations, and 'narratives for the stories/values of all stakeholders' (p. 23). Marshall further stresses the value of research that 'creates a relationship with individuals and respects their meaning-making' and the development of research agendas that explore the 'areas of silence and non-events, the counter-narratives and counterpublics' (p. 23). Her calls make even messier the project for inclusion as suggested by the research reported here, but nonetheless signal the shift in conceptualising the scale of a project that is always beginning and will never be finished.

Notes

1. In state folklore a symbol is adopted by each state such that Kansas is known as the Sunflower State, New Mexico as the Land of Enchantment, and New York as the Empire State.
2. In a later project on school-linked service integration, I in fact, implemented a cross-dialogue design with teachers, parents, agency directors, and school social workers in a federally-funded project (Ware 1996a, 1997a, 1997b, 1997c).
3. Dual-license programs are prevalent in the US as a bureaucratic solution to the separate certification requirements for teachers as either general or special education teachers. In a dual-license program a teacher is certified to teach in either general or special education classrooms following the completion of additional coursework. The irony being that universities continue to offer separate certification programmes in addition to the dual-license certificate.
4. The Consent Decree specifically pertained to timely evaluation, programme recommendations and placements; full parental involvement in meetings of the Committee on Special Education (CSE) and in other aspects of their children's special education; education in the least restrictive environment and a reduction in the number of students with disabilities placed on home instruction; equal access by students with disabilities to the District's special schools and programmes, curriculum and extracurricular activities, and school facilities, equipment and supplies; and a self-monitoring system which the District itself could use to monitor and maintain compliance.

5. The models for inclusion are the blended classroom which combines two complete age-appropriate general and special education classrooms, and is instructed by two teachers (one general and one special education) with a total class size maintained at the general education limit (33 maximum) plus the special education limit (15 maximum). The modified blended classroom which is a special education class divided among two to three age-appropriate general education classrooms, instructed by the general and special education teacher who divide their time between two to three classrooms, with a total class size maintained at the general education limit (33 maximum). And the individual placement where students with disabilities are placed in age-appropriate general education classrooms in numbers no greater than those that would occur in natural proportions in the District, and where instruction is provided by the general education teacher in consultation with special education personnel with class sizes maintained at the general education limit

Chapter 5

'Vive la différence?' Exploring context, policy and change in special education in France: developing cross-cultural collaboration

Felicity Armstrong, Brigitte Belmont and Aliette Verillon

Introduction

This chapter forms part of discussion and collaboration between the authors over the past four years. It explores issues relating to difference, disability and equality in education in the light of recent developments in policy making in France. But it is also about cross-cultural enquiry in that we shall try to draw out some of the issues and contradictions which have emerged in the process of our collaboration.

One difficulty which we have encountered in attempting to write a chapter together is in finding a common voice and – at the same time – distinguishing between the 'we' and the 'I'. How is it possible to write a chapter *together* when we have such different cultural perspectives and experiences? These differences have made our discussions exciting and challenging, and one important outcome of our research has been a heightened awareness of the struggles and contradictions within the research process itself, as well as within education systems. Would an attempt to 'write with one voice' iron out these differences and contradictions which have enriched our discussions, imposing a 'sanitised and clinical voice' (Harris 1999) over the clamour of competing perspectives which have emerged in the process of our discussions? Or would one person's perspective take precedence over those of the other authors, overriding their voices? What issues are raised when 'outsiders' attempt to observe and analyse contexts and cultures which are not 'their own'? Shouldn't the voice of 'insiders' always take precedence over those of 'outsiders'? But isn't there also a danger of giving particular authenticity to insider voices as somehow representing a particular cultural community, when in fact they can only represent their own individual perspective? These are real issues for us, especially as the English author has translated some sections written by her French colleagues – notably the sections on historical and recent policy developments – and these form an important part of this chapter. This makes the issues of interpretation and accuracy particularly central to the process of collaborative writing. Of course, many of these issues arise in any jointly authored work; different cultural perspectives and experiences are not just a feature of different nationalities.

All these questions have made the writing of this chapter a creative challenge, but it has also opened up for scrutiny the process of collaboration as well as raising questions about our own assumptions and values and the cultural and political meanings we give to concepts such as equality, policy and rights.

The chapter opens with some reflections on cross-cultural research, especially in the context of 'special education' in France, involving both the 'insider' perspectives of Aliette Verillon and Brigitte Belmont, and an 'outsider' perspective from England, Felicity Armstrong.

The second section outlines the historical development of special education in France, focusing in particular on policy and equality issues. In the third section recent policy developments and some of the contradictions which have emerged in relation to issues of inclusion and exclusion and stated policies favouring 'integration' are discussed. The final section draws out some observations and questions which have arisen from our collaborative work and will return to issues relating to cross-cultural enquiry and understandings concerning notions of 'equality' and 'policy'.

Cross-cultural research in special education

Particular difficulties are raised when trying to discuss education systems across cultures. First of all, terminology poses major problems because there are important differences in the perceptions, responses and processes of naming and categorisation in different cultures (Booth 1995). There is also the related problem of translating words, phrases and terminology used in one language into another. How can we be certain that the translation respects cultural values and meanings? Yet, finding an exact translation of terminology – if such a thing is possible – would not resolve the ideological issues. We need, then, to look beyond the ways in which disabilities are officially categorised, counted and legitimated, beyond the language used to talk about them, beyond the institutions which are an integral part of these processes, to the practices and values which underlie, and operate through, social systems.

A further problem arises in trying to compare, or find common ground for talking about, different structures, procedures and institutions. For example, the structures, practices and institutions which have been developed as social responses to, and constructions of, difference and disability in France and the UK are difficult to compare. In France not all provision for children and young people is made within the education system. Some attend establishments run by the Ministry of Social, Urban and Health Services rather than Education which makes it difficult to talk about 'special education' as if it were a single structure under the control of the Ministry of Education (Armstrong 1995b, in Potts, Armstrong and Masterton 1995). For these reasons, it is hard to draw parallels or clear contrasts between education systems.

Inclusion, exclusion and integration

In France as in the the UK, the term 'integration' is used loosely to refer to arrangements which increase participation or contact between a disabled pupil or pupils enrolled in some form of segregated provision and those in mainstream educational settings. While the term 'exclusion' is widely used and understood in France to refer to political and social processes which discriminate against and exclude groups in the context of work, social, economic, cultural and educational opportunities and participation (e.g. Paugam 1996), the term *inclusion* has hardly been used in this context. This has made a discussion of the terms 'inclusion' and 'integration' complex and difficult. It has also brought about changes in the ways we have understood the term 'exclusion'. The strong French concept of exclusion has revealed the limitations of the British application of the term which traditionally has referred only to pupils who were physically excluded from school or excluded *within* schools through narrow curricula and intolerant cultures and practices (although recently New Labour has adopted the struggle against 'social exclusion' as part of its discourse). The term *intégration* is sometimes used in French in ways which are similar to the recent wider use of the term *inclusion* in England in relation to social policy:

> The notion of inclusion (*intégration*) refers to social values which are commonly accepted and are not only concerned with disabled people. We refer to the inclusion (*intégration*) of immigrant groups, to inclusion (*intégration*) of unemployed young people into the work-force, and the fight against social exclusion experienced through unemployment. So the notion of inclusion (*intégration*) concerns the recognition of the right of all individuals to full participation in social life as full and participating actors. (Belmont and Verillon 1997, translated from French)

While any discussion of policy and equality in education must be placed in a broad social context, the example of France points to the dangers of making assumptions about particular social institutions and practices on the basis of the more general context. Thus, for example, in France the wider debate concerning the nature of social exclusion and measures to prevent it (or neutralise its damaging effects), has not really begun to penetrate the arena of special education. Debate concerning social exclusions and the construction of difference in French society (Stiker 1996) continues to be mainly disconnected from the entrenched structural, physical, attitudinal and curricular segregation of disabled children whose origins are deeply rooted in the medical model.

Structures, institutions and procedures

The second area of difficulty concerns differences in the structures and institutions between countries and is well exemplified when comparing France and the UK.

Education systems exert social and ideological control over society in complex and contradictory ways through institutionalised processes of selection, categorisation and segregation as well as through the curriculum and practices of teaching and learning (Apple 1995). Hegemonic control is achieved by one class or group establishing social and cultural leadership over other groups. The hegemonic role of education is expressed through organisational mechanisms such as the ways in which pupils are grouped for learning, the content of the curriculum and the social relationships established in educational institutions. This argument provides a framework for understanding the complex relationships involved in the ways in which societies identify and respond to pupils labelled as 'having special educational needs', 'handicapped', 'in difficulty', and so forth.

The systems which select pupils for special educational treatment are an integral part of the processes of selection and segregation in the broader educational system. Bourdieu and Passeron (1977) described the way the systems of selection by examination serve to reproduce social relationships:

> Nothing is better designed than the examination to inspire universal recognition of the legitimacy of academic verdicts and of the social hierarchies they legitimate, since it leads the self-eliminated to count themselves among those who fail ... (Bourdieu and Passeron 1977, p. 162)

This text referred to the formal examination systems which exist inside the ordinary French education system, but the argument can be extended to include all systems of examination and assessment including processes of medical examination, multi-professional assessment, the deliberations and decisions made by 'commissions' or multi-professional assessment panels, psychological testing and all the other examinations which exist to categorise, select, and exclude and treat pupils in both France and the UK. In France the gates of the ordinary 'école maternelle' are wide, with nearly 99 per cent of three year olds attending nursery school. By the secondary school stage there is a decrease in the range of provision within the education system and there is a corresponding increase in the numbers of young people in segregated special institutions. This appears to be in sharp contrast to many other countries where the trend is the other way (OECD 1995). An important reason for this is the existence of the parallel systems of education and quasi-medical provision (Armstrong 1995a, 1995b, 1996, Plaisance 1996, Vial 1990). Although there has been legislation passed in Parliament designed to widen participation in education, the principle features of the state education apparatus have remained in place, such as the vast and complex system of médico-éducatif institutions which filter off many young people from the education system. Thus large numbers are excluded from ordinary social, educational and cultural experiences, legitimating a culture of segregation and mystique around difference.

Historical context

Questions relating to equality and citizenship concerning disabled people emerged following the French Revolution at the end of the eighteenth century. While the republican (and revolutionary) demand that the education system should be based on principles of equality has been clearly discernible in government discourse, historically this principle has been confused with a strong liberal-humanitarian commitment to providing special, segregating provision for disabled children. During this period numerous asylums were built to accommodate sick and disabled people, those who were destitute, 'delinquents' and others cast out by society. The main purpose of the asylums was to 'protect' both the rest of society and those whom they contained, as well as having a moral role in purifying and imposing order (Foucault 1967, Scull 1979).

The eighteenth century, 'the Age of Enlightenment', was characterised by a marked change in scientific and philosophical thinking which changed perceptions about human beings and their relationships within society. For the first time work was begun to investigate the 'educability' of children who had previously been considered incapable of learning anything. L' Abbé de l'Epée began his work with deaf children in 1774 and Haüy began teaching blind children in 1786. This was followed by teaching experiments by Itard with children labelled as 'idiots' in contemporary discourse. This work and that of other thinkers began to change attitudes in society. People who had been literally cast out from society and regarded as ineducable and useless were now perceived as capable of developing behaviour and skills which would allow them to belong and contribute in ordinary society.

As ideas concerning equality and democracy strengthened, ideas emerged concerning the right to assistance for all those in need and the right to some form of instruction for all 'in order to offer them the means to provide to meet their needs, to assure their well-being, to know and be able to exercise their rights, to understand and be able to fulfil their duties' (Condorcet 1792).

Later, doctors such as Bourneville (1906/1907), working in the context of hospitals, fought in vain for schooling for 'backward' pupils to take place in classes attached to ordinary schools. Special classes called 'remedial classes' were first set up in 1909, but places in them were filled by pupils who were already in school but experiencing difficulties and were labelled as 'anormaux d'école' (Binet and Simon 1907). (A possible translation for this term might be 'abnormal pupils'.)

One response to the shortage of provision for young disabled people was the creation of 'médico-éducatif' establishments. These institutions were often set up through the initiatives of private associations of parents. They grouped children together according to the label ascribed to them on the basis of medical classifications, with the purpose of offering them the particular specialist intervention and educational programmes adapted in response to particular impairments.

In the early 1970s, carried forward on a groundswell of thinking and debate opposed to incarceration in psychiatric asylums, social marginalisation and stigmatisation, policies relating to the education of disabled children began to change. Ordinary schools, it was argued, should be regarded as the most appropriate educational settings for all children. By providing disabled children with the same conditions for learning and social development as other children, they would be more easily integrated into ordinary social life later on. Integration was seen – and still is – as enhancing equality of opportunity.

The 1975 law (the *loi d'orintation en faveur des personnes handicapées*) introduced compulsory education for disabled children, including them for the first time in provision 'as a right'. The same law also gave disabled children the 'right' to attend an ordinary school 'if their level of aptitude made this possible' (dans la mèsure où 'leurs aptitudes le permettent'). However, the law left intact the powerful system of special schools and medical institution which exist *outside* the education system, providing a historically sanctioned and familiar alternative to ordinary education. The 1989 Law (the loi Jospin) introduced changes in primary education which were designed to recognise and respond to the broad diversity of children represented in French primary schools. This marked a change in emphasis: difference and diversity and a need for greater flexibility in curriculum and teaching were acknowledged. While the 1989 Act did not focus primarily on children with learning difficulties or disabilities, it did represent a change in orientation and passed more control to teachers over how and what they taught. This was seen as favouring integration for a greater number of children.

Recent policy developments

In France children identified as experiencing – or deemed likely to experience – educational difficulties are divided into two broad categories: disabled children, and those who experience difficulties in learning. Underpinning this distinction is the principle that children can be grouped together on the basis of categories of impairment for the purposes of policy making, and are perceived as requiring different educational experiences and opportunities than other children unless they can fit in to existing structures and practices (the term 'handicap' continues to be used).

Within this deficit model, some changes have taken place in recent years, notably the abandonment of the notion of 'debility', replacing it with the term 'mental retardation' in accordance with the World Health Organisation (WHO) 'International Classification of Impairment, Disability and Handicap' (ICIDH) published in 1980. This internationally sanctioned taxonomy of impairment, based on definitions which are 'reducible to individual and biological pathology' (Oliver and Barnes 1998, p. 17), ostensibly intended to provide greater coherence and simplify the meanings attached to categorisation across contexts, has been treated as somehow beyond the reaches of critique and as a 'gold standard' against which children can be tested, measured and assigned particular labels. As such, it is a powerful agent in preserving disabling practices and exclusions.

The uncontested use of the WHO classification and processes of assessment and categorisation of children according to impairment-led procedures have now been expanded to include observation of the child to assess their 'developmental potential'. Greater emphasis is placed on the child's performance and projected future development, and less on the 'origin' of their difficulties. This view, while seeming to take into account the importance of context in evaluating a child's development, still places the *origins* of such difficulties within the child. In effect, it positions the professional gaze even more powerfully than ever before in relation to disabled children and their families.

However, this change in emphasis has had some impact on educational practices. In the past, the belief that cognitive difficulties were irreversible and insurmountable was linked to the provision of special, segregated provision for many children for whom educational objectives were limited and prescribed. Current thinking has moved towards an acceptance that, within the educational system, the aims of education for disabled children should be 'the same' as those for other children. What this means within a highly centralised and formalised system of education in which historically 'equality' has been understood as children receiving identical curricula and pedagogy, regardless of differences between them, is a subject for debate. The realisation of this principle, it is argued, must involve the adaptation of curricula and teaching practices so that disabled children have access to the same curriculum as other pupils and that expectations about individual attainment should not be prescribed on the basis of perceived ability or disability. As in England, such a process is far from being realised.

France has not adopted the term 'special educational needs' uncritically (Courteix 1999), and there is currently an important debate going on in relation to values and terminology in the face of the variety of discourses, polices and practices in countries in the rest of Europe. The use of the term 'special educational needs', adopted by England and Wales and enshrined in the Warnock Report (DES 1978) and in the 1981 Education Act, has been questioned on a number of counts. Firstly, it is argued that the use of this term is itself stigmatising because it identifies certain children as in need of particular measures which mark them out as different from other children. Secondly, the term 'special educational needs' has itself become a homogenising, deficit mega-category, replacing earlier deficit categories – or masking their continued use. As such, the use of this term does not challenge existing perceptions and stereotypes, nor does it contribute to a positive critique of current policies and practices which might lead to the development of more equitable responses to individual differences in relation to teaching and learning. The term 'specific educational needs' is commonly used in the context of ordinary schools, but medical labels are still part of the culture, and one basis for important organisation and decision making, in special education settings.

Responding to difference

In primary education, children who experience difficulties in learning (but who are not categorised as 'disabled') are supported in their learning in ordinary schools through the Réseaux d'Aides Specialisées aux Enfants en Difficultés – or RASED – (Special Support Network for Children in Difficulty). The aim of these structures is to adapt or change the educational conditions and experience for pupils who are deemed to have difficulties by providing support and intervention to individual pupils or groups of pupils. In principle, the RASED should also provide support for pupils who, in the past, would have been placed in special remedial classes based in ordinary schools ('classes de perfectionnement') which were closed down in 1991. Many children placed in those classes experienced difficulties in school which related to 'intellectual impairment'.

Disabled children either attend a special school full time, or participate in an integration project in an ordinary school. Pupils may be integrated either on an individual basis in an ordinary class, or as a group of pupils who make up special classes based in ordinary schools.

Integration projects for individual children depend upon the involvement of specialist services coming into the ordinary school from outside.

In 1991 Classes d'Intégration Scolaire – CLIS – (Integration Classes) were introduced in order to facilitate 'collective integration' of groups of pupils according to impairment. Pupils who attend the CLIS have been assessed by a *Commission d'Éducation Special* (Special Education Commission), as 'not being able to benefit from' integration in an ordinary class but not requiring provision in a special school. The introduction of the CLIS represents the moving of the sites of particular specialist, segregated provision from the outside to the inside of the ordinary education system. In this sense, special education, while maintaining segregated specialist structures and practices outside ordinary schools, is also being re-articulated inside ordinary schools. There are four different kinds of CLIS which are differentiated on the basis of the following impairments: visual, hearing, physical disability and learning difficulty which is sub-divided to include the category of 'mental handicap'. Teachers who work in CLIS must have undertaken specialist impairment-related training as well as being qualified and experienced teachers in ordinary schools. In theory, the CLIS do not function independently, but as part of the life of the ordinary classes in the school. Pupils should share the same learning activities and opportunities in ordinary classes. However, in practice this 'principle' is articulated only through recommendations rather than statutory regulations, and the reality – as revealed by a 1995 Ministry of Education General Inspection – is very different from the principle.

Particular dilemmas are raised by the categorisation procedures on which the special education system is based. Two such dilemmas are, firstly, that teachers feel that they are not equipped to teach, in the mainstream setting, children who would, in the past, have been in segregated special classes. Secondly, there have been difficulties associated with categorisation within the broad category of 'learning difficulty', notably distinguishing between 'mental handicap' and 'difficulties in learning'. The criteria are vague, making decisions based on them almost random. This acknowledgement of the subjective nature of such procedures raises questions about their usefulness either in bureaucratic terms, or in terms of their use for purposes other than for those for which they are systematically presented.

Educational provision is therefore variable and uneven. While remedial, segregated classes no longer exist in some areas, in others they continue to be used. Although some classes are called Classes d'Intégration Scolaire, the pupils are categorised according to the same criteria as those who attended remedial classes in the past. There has been considerable difficulty, too, in breaking down the barriers between the CLIS and ordinary classes and the participation of disabled pupils in learning activities with their peers is exceptional. 'Integration' remains a function of 'non academic' activities such as playtime or lunch.

While in theory the CLIS are supposed to provide disabled children with the opportunity for integration, the categorisation and grouping of disabled pupils according to impairment affirms the notion that their needs are so great and so particular that they can only be met by highly trained specialists. Such a representation presents particular barriers to collaboration between specialist teachers whose work is associated with the CLIS and their colleagues who work in the wider school setting and prevents the development of participation and inclusion of disabled children in learning activities with their peers.

Indeed, as long as the term 'special' or 'specialised' is used in ways which mark out and separate one group of learners from another, exclusions will continue to be integral and defining processes in the education system. 'Special' is part of an exclusionary discourse, symbolising the wider social processes that deny equality of opportunity for full social and educational participation for all children regardless of difference. An understanding of the role of discourse as an integral part of policy making,

> means putting policy in a political framework and locating it in a wider model of social life as consisting of discursive social practices: we act on the basis of our discourse about an aspect of the social world, such as whether we divide schoolchildren into those with disabilities and those without, or whether we see all schoolchildren, firstly, as pupils. (Fulcher 1989, p. 15)

Secondary education

Students transfer from primary school to the *collège* at the age of 11, where they spend four years. In this first stage of secondary education students are channelled either in the direction of an academic route or a vocational route, according to judgements made about their abilities through processes of selection at the age of 13. This marks a break with the primary phase in which children who attend ordinary classes in primary schools share a common curriculum as part of the republican ideal of equality. Pupils who continue to experience difficulties after transition from the primary stage are placed in special classes under the remit of the *sections d'enseignement général et professionnel adapté* (General and adapted professional training sections) – or 'SEGPA'. In these classes, which are attached to ordinary secondary schools, teaching methods are expected to respond to pupil diversity and a range of learning styles, as far as possible, with the aim of supporting students in acquiring recognised professional training and qualifications as well as providing a general education. Unlike most other European countries, in France the proportion of disabled pupils who attend ordinary schools is even lower at secondary level than at the primary level (OECD 1995).

Policy making and integration

The 1975 law made education for all children a legal requirement, but 'integration' is not a statutory requirement or obligation on the part of the education system. 'Integration' into ordinary schools is presented as being an important aim which policy makers, education officers and schools should be working towards, rather than a policy that has the force of law.

This position implies that while 'integration' is a clearly audible stated policy, there are clearly visible alternative solutions. Policy making in France does not challenge the existence and the legitimacy of a segregated system of special education in which economic stakes are powerfully entrenched and is rooted in a long history of the development of highly differentiated, medically oriented structures, and which remain an alternative, parallel system. The powerful, continuing presence of segregated provision sanctions the perpetuation of the exclusion of thousands of children from ordinary schools on the grounds of learning difficulty or disability.

Integration in all its different forms is unevenly applied and is only adopted when it is judged to be 'in the child's best educational interests'. This criteria leaves open the alternative possibility of deciding in favour of special, segregated provision. Such decision making rests on the judgements, attitudes and possible interests of those involved in assessment and evaluation procedures in relation to particular children in local contexts.

Even when a decision has been made to develop an integration project for a particular child or group of children, this is not a firm or permanent or certain project which will be developed with the ultimate aim of achieving full inclusion as a right. Integration projects are monitored and reviewed, to allow adjustments to be made in the kind and level of support offered to the child, and in the modification of curriculum and pedagogy. But the evaluation process also leaves open alternative provision in the form of a placement in – or return to – a segregated special school if the integration project is not judged to be 'a success'.

Integration is itself 'exclusionary' in that it is not offered to all disabled children, being reserved only to those who are perceived as being able to 'benefit' and capable of making the necessary adaptations to life in an ordinary school. This accords legitimacy to the profoundly discriminatory assumption of a hierarchy of impairment and sustains an 'underclass' of excluded children and young people. To be admitted to an ordinary school, the child must meet certain conditions. These include:

> The ability to communicate.
> The ability to participate in the socialisation processes expected in the ordinary school.

> The ability to make progress in learning in ways which are compatible with the curriculum and learning requirements of the ordinary school. (Ministry of Education Circular, No. 91–302, 1991)

Far from breaking down exclusionary and inequitable practices, these requirements constitute a series of tests which provide barriers to inclusion.

Although there is an expressed concern in policy documents and current debate with the 'best interests' of the child, the greatest attention and emphasis is still placed on perceptions about the child's difficulties and judgements made about the child's ability to 'adapt' and 'benefit', rather than on the social and political demand for schools to change, and curriculum and pedagogy to be re-defined and made more flexible so that all learners are included.

Only those children who are regarded as conforming to the dominant 'norms' in terms of communication, socialisation and learning are likely to be considered suitable candidates for integration. A perceived 'gap' between a child's attainment and that of other children in the class is seen as indicating removal to special, segregated provision. Schools, then, only accommodate very narrow variations in attainment and performance, thus restricting 'integration'. 'Inclusion' represents a very different, and opposed, paradigm to that represented by current policy making concerning the purposes of education and the discriminatory role of selection in preserving existing social relations and divisions.

Policies are subject to the interpretations and 'goodwill' of the actors involved in different contexts for their realisation. The 'actors' include:

- teachers in schools
- the planners, officers and inspectors of the state national education system who have considerable power in interpreting and implementing policy and whose views and perceptions play a powerful role in promoting, or impeding, change
- those involved in the complex, parallel system of segregated special education who respond to and interpret policy making in relation to integration and collaboration with ordinary schools in different ways, reflecting differences in personal and professional perspectives and interests
- parents who can exert considerable power through the *associations* (parental organisations which are important lobbying and consciousness raising bodies).

These groups are far from homogeneous. In the case of all these groups of actors the degree to which willingness and resistance play a role in relation to breaking down barriers between special and ordinary education is crucial. As in most countries, children's voices appear to be marginalised in decision-making procedures relating to their education. This *willingness* or *resistance* presents serious problems in terms of achieving continuity in provision. Difficulties arise particularly when 'integration' is not conceived as being a school project involving all teachers and pupils and when an 'integrated' child moves from one class to another and the new class teacher is not willingly engaged in the project.

Integration or inclusion?

Integraton and inclusion represent two opposing political goals. The argument that integration is a stage on the pathway leading towards inclusion – that it is a 'less developed' version of inclusion – fails to recognise that *integration* reproduces and emphasises differences in that, far from challenging practices of segregation, it is concerned with technical arrangements for allowing some children to attend ordinary schools on the basis of selection. The fundamental principle underpinning inclusive education is that schools are for all members of the community, that they are part of – and serve – that community, without exception.

The current stated aim of policy making in France is to adapt the present education system so that it responds to 'children's needs'. The 1989 Education Act *recommends* differentiation through teaching to respond to diversity. A stated purpose of this recommendation is to encourage integration of disabled children. But the demands made on the education system to change are very limited and reflect an acceptance that some children will be excluded from it. Furthermore, underpining the mechanisms through which 'integration' takes place is the conception of 'adaptation' as being concerned with providing specific support to individual disabled children rather than being concerned with bringing about change in the cultures and practices of schools, involving the whole school community.

Research carried out by Brigitte Belmont and Aliette Verillon (Lantier *et al.* 1994, Belmont and Verillon 1999) suggests that innovations in teaching and modifications in curricula and pedagogy relating to individual integration projects are potentially beneficial to all children in the class, regardless of disability or learning difficulty. Certain difficulties in learning commonly ascribed to children on the basis of impairment, are no different from difficulties experienced by other pupils in the class. While certain technical adjustments or installations may be necessary to overcome environmental barriers to learning, there is nothing very specific about the requirements of disabled children in terms of their learning which mark them out from their peers. All children benefit from participating in a stimulating learning environment in which individual differences and learning styles are taken into account and time is given for questioning, experimentation, discussion and collaborative working.

While adopting a rhetoric of 'schools for all', official policy documents do not include any fundamental re-assessment of the education system with the aim of transforming it so that schools welcome all children on an equal basis and this represents a fundamental contradiction. On the one hand, the official stated political aim is of developing innovative approaches to teaching and learning so as to take into account pupil diversity. On the other, the principle of special, individualised and separate treatment of learning difficulties within the ordinary school and the continued existence of a monolithic parallel system of special schools remain largely unchallenged.

Children continue to be assessed, categorised and placed according to perceptions about the 'problems' which *they cause* because of perceived disability, learning difficulty or some other category of within-child deficit which deny the richness and diversity of human experience.

In a declaration made by the Ministry of Education (February 1999), a particular concern was expressed about the failure to develop a system of integration which meets parental demands. (Current assessments suggest that only one disabled child in three attends an ordinary school, many of whom are in separate, special classes.) Measures have been announced which are intended to strengthen integration initiatives through changes in professional development for teachers, and the employment of young support assistants ('aides-éducateurs'). These measures are concerned with increasing the levels of 'integration' and in no way address the much greater project of creating an inclusive system of education. While principles underpining inclusive education are in direct opposition to those underpining integration, there is much to be learnt from the experience of integration, both about teaching and learning, and about the political nature and effects of policy making. Education policies based on principles of equality for all challenge the state because they evoke

> rights which are opposed to the principles which underpin 'rights' accorded by the state. An example of this can be found in the opposing values which underpin the idea of 'integration' and the principle of inclusive education. Integration is based on a particular kind of rationality, referring to the 'right' of disabled children to attend their local schools provided the 'rights' of others are not threatened ... (Armstrong and Barton 1999b, p. 215)

Like the notion of integration underpining the UK 1981 Act, integration as represented in legislation and policy and as it is realised through practice, is contingent, provisional and dependent upon principles relating to perceptions of efficiency, performance and measurable outcomes. Inclusive education is concerned with the human right for *all* children to attend their local school. Such a principle is in fundamental conflict with principles of integration and with the state because it is based on the principle that all members of society should be treated equally. Of course, societies whose stated policies favour 'equality' have interpreted this concept in different ways at different historical periods. Thus in France and England the provision of custodial environments set up to care for and protect vulnerable people were, at the time, seen as offering equality in terms of the right to subsistence, care and protection based on the assumption that these were commonly enjoyed by the rest of society.

Policy making and change

At the centre of our discussion is the nature of policy and how policies are made. In France, formal policy making is still profoundly influenced by the historic narratives of liberty, fraternity and equality which emerged from the French Revolution of 1789, as well as the establishment of strong centralised government during the Napoleonic period. The state exerts a strong controlling role over all services relating to social life such as education and health, with the declared aim of ensuring order and equity. Legislation passed to increase participation of disabled children and young people in education and in ordinary schools is part of this project. The varied interpretation of government policies in different arenas and the often contradictory relationship *between* policies, have confused and interrupted attempts to introduce change. An example of this is the contradiction between policies which speak in favour of greater participation in ordinary schools on the one hand, and the traditional inflexibility in classroom practice arising from centrally imposed curricula and pedagogy. Paradoxically, these policies both have their origins in a stated concern with principles of equality of opportunity. The 'school for all' is part of the French republican ideal and, as attitudes have changed towards disabled people, demands for greater participation in all arenas of social life have increased. Yet, the principle that all children should receive 'the same' curriculum and teaching, regardless of difference, has in the past delayed creative innovation and flexibility in educational practice which is needed if schools are to change. This, to some extent, explains the perseveration of the idea that children must adapt, rather than schools. This argument, while reducing some very complex issues and contests to some rather simple statements, points to some of the struggles and connections between education policy making and historical context and social change. But, as Ball (1994) argues,

> any decent theory of education policy must not be limited to a state control perspective. Policy is an 'economy of power', a set of technologies and practices which are realized and struggled over in local settings. Policy is both text and action, words and deeds, it is what is enacted as well as what is intended ... Policies are always incomplete

insofar as they relate to or map on to the 'wild profusion' of local practice. (Ball 1994, pp. 10–11)

Out of the struggles and contradictions are emerging open national debate, innovation and research based on the need for change and the question: what kind of education system do we want to have? There is currently a different, but overlapping, national debate going on concerning the future of secondary schools in urban areas, in which student disaffection has sometimes led to a breakdown of trust and security, leading to strikes and closures. Underpinning this debate are the questions: who are schools for? what kind of society are we to build for the future? Linked to this debate is the work of researchers at, for example, the Centre de Recherche de L'Éducation Spécialisée et de l'Adaptation Scolaire (Institut National de Recherche Pédagogique, Paris) into education practices and marginalisation (Cohen and Hugon 1995) and a wider questioning of values and processes in education at all levels. This work is all part of the complex processes involved in policy making which, as Fulcher (1993) argues in Slee (1993),

> dissolves ... distinctions between theory, policy, practice – arguing against the top-down model of policy and the idea of implementation – and putting policy in a wider model of social life as social practice ... (Fulcher 1993, in Slee 1993, p. 129).

The task of cross-cultural collaboration

In writing this chapter, our discussions have involved us in a close examination of the concepts and terminology which we use and draw on in our different cultural contexts. We have had to unravel and argue about how we understand and interpret notions of equality and inclusion and how these are interpreted through practice in our different settings. In doing so, we have had to grapple with some of the complexities and contradictions involved in cross-cultural research through trying to understand the cultures and perspectives of others. Following Tony Booth and Mel Ainscow,

> we regard the task of uncovering the nature of perspectives and the way they are culturally and politically constrained as an essential step in learning from the practices of others. (Booth and Ainscow 1998, p. 2)

At the same time, we must acknowledge and try to understand the diversity, contradictions and power relations which exist within societies, as well as between them. Representations of cultures and populations as homogeneous, sharing common perspectives and understandings, are constructs which serve to oil the wheels of flimsy comparative work.

Initial divisions or differences between us which have emerged during the process of debate have not been drawn up according to national boundaries. We have come to resist talking as if we expect each other to adhere to particular perspectives represented, say, in national government policies, and we have become critically watchful to avoid slippage into simplistic generalisations.

What have we learned from collaborative research and debate? First, to develop a curiosity for the 'foreign' and – in turn – to experience the curiousness of practices in our own cultures. Through cross-cultural debate we may discover the 'oddness of the ordinary' (Sibley 1995) in familiar landscapes which is

> about making what is strange familiar and what is familiar strange, like seeing your own town in a new light when showing a visitor around. Features that are normally ignored become clearer, possibilities that have been overlooked are reconsidered, and things that have been taken for granted are subject to new scrutiny. (Booth and Ainscow 1998, p. 5)

Isn't it *odd* that drugs such as Ritalin are administered to children in England to control their behaviour in school? This practice is illegal in France and anathema to teachers' perceptions of human rights. And how *odd* that some schools, both in England and France, should exclude young women for wearing the hijab?

In cross-cultural work *listening* and *seeing* become key research tools – almost methodologies. By engaging and refining listening and seeing it becomes possible to begin to understand different cultures, systems and meanings.

Cross-cultural enquiry allows us to work in naïve ways and ask simple and direct questions. We can, for example, ask questions such as: What does the concept of 'equality' mean in the context of the practices and values of ordinary schools in France and England? Are principles of equality and fairness applied to all members of the community in education? How do the values and practices in local communities relate to those in schools? Which groups are excluded in education, and what forms do these exclusions take? Why do disabled children go to segregated schools or units? Or, Why are many children routinely labelled as having 'emotional and behavioural difficulties' in England and why does this label often trigger their removal from ordinary schools? (Why indeed? In France children whose behaviour causes concern are very rarely excluded from their schools; practices in England in this sphere provoke bewilderment in France.)

Being 'naïve' entails an understanding that every word, use of terminology, concept, value, statement, process needs to be carefully considered, looked at from different perspectives, challenged and discussed. Nothing can be taken for granted. Shared meanings can never be assumed.

In turn, this openness of mind, this critical gaze can be swivelled round and turned on to ordinary, familiar landscapes which we think we know, throwing them into sharp relief, changing relationships and meanings, provoking new questions. We make the familiar strange by looking at our own cultures through the eyes of others.

We wish to thank Philip Armstrong, Len Barton, Tony Booth, Suzy Harris and Pierre Verillon for reading and commenting on our chapter.

Chapter 6

Inclusion and exclusion policy in England: who controls the agenda?

Tony Booth

Terms of engagement

In this chapter I will consider some aspects of inclusion policy in England. I define inclusive education as the process of increasing the participation of learners within and reducing their exclusion from, the cultures, curricula and communities of neighbourhood centres of learning (Booth 1996). I have begun to experiment with calling this project 'inclusion/exclusion' to keep these dimensions at the forefront of our minds. It is concerned with the careful fostering of a mutually sustaining relationship between local centres of learning and all members of their surrounding communities. It is about giving learners an equality of regard irrespective of their background, gender, ethnicity, sexuality, disability and attainment.

In the English context, inclusion/exclusion can be identified, with the development of *comprehensive* community preschool, school and further (post 16) education. It is concerned with the removal of barriers to participation in 'one school (or other education centre) for all'. It is about who, from the surrounding communities, attends a particular learning centre and the nature and quality of his or her participation within it. It is about all forms of selection within and between schools, and the identification and minimising of all barriers to learning and participation.

Notions of inclusion/exclusion become strained in further education because of the fragmentation of the student population and their courses. And the extent to which we see higher education as available to all or reserved for an élite tests the limits to our view of educational inclusion. Typically in higher education there has been a concern with removing barriers to access and participation for students and staff because of their background, sexuality, gender, disability and ethnicity but not unconditionally because of their attainment. Though in institutions such as the Open University, in England, *access* has been open to almost all.

I do not see educational inclusion as concerned primarily with disabled children and young people or with learners categorised as 'having special educational needs'. I do not think we can take an inclusion project very far if it is framed in such exclusive terms. Within England and internationally such a view obscures excluding pressures based on wealth, ethnicity, gender, sexuality, class and attainment. A narrow view of inclusion concedes the inclusion agenda to central government, and hides the exclusionary force of a competitive system of education in which schools are seen as failing corner shops or successful supermarkets. It restricts our thinking and blunts our critique. We cannot include others, or ourselves, in education unless we speak our own words.

A political process

I regard inclusion/exclusion, essentially, as a political process. Possibilities for, and barriers to, inclusion are shaped by all aspects of education and social policy – not just by policies that carry an inclusion label. Such a view is well represented in the *International Journal of Inclusive Education*. Further, inclusion/exclusion is only part of an endeavour to reduce exclusion within society more generally. In 1983, I defined 'integration' as the process of 'increasing the participation of people in their communities' to reflect this concern with all social contexts. Giddens (1999) has suggested that inclusion has become synonymous with equality and exclusion with inequality. In relating inclusion and exclusion to issues of equality I would prefer to give them more active meanings, as the 'reduction of inequality' and the 'increase of inequality', respectively.

Reconnecting education and social policy

Education is a primary means of effecting social policy but such a connection is lost where governments view education solely as a technology for raising the performance of individuals and the economy. The method for increasing learner achievement is seen as the discovery and implementation of 'what works' in schools. Such a notion leads politicians to ignore the social consequences of education policies both inside and outside schools. Thus we have a policy of 'naming and shaming' failing schools and teachers, identified during school inspections, that rivals the excesses of the Chinese Cultural Revolution. The Secretary of State for Education is at pains to defend these policies, and to ignore the effects they have on teaching and learning communities, because he believes they will push up standards (*TES*, 14 November 1997, p. 1). Yet ultimately, as Michael Fielding (1999) argues so compellingly, achievements mean nothing if it is not seen in the context of school communities that enhance the spirit of teachers and learners.

A further illustration of the disconnection of education policies from their social effects is provided by the work of the 'social exclusion unit' linked to the Cabinet Office. It develops policy discussion papers about the reduction of marginalisation in society. In the 'national strategy for neighbourhood renewal' (Social Exclusion Unit 1998) there is a recognition of the damaging effect that some government policies might have on neighbourhoods:

> Past Government policies have also often contributed to the problem. Poor housing design has had a big impact, weakening communities and making neighbourhoods less safe. And policies on housing allocation, rents and benefits have tended to concentrate the poor and unemployed together in neighbourhoods where hardly anyone has a job. (Social Exclusion Unit 1998, Summary, para. 5)

However, the widely reported negative effects on neighbourhood cohesion of government education policies are ignored within the report (see Power and Mumford 1999). A concern to examine the nature of inclusive school cultures and their implications for the relationship between schools and their communities can help to highlight the significance of education in increasing social cohesion or disintegration.

A comparative perspective

In writing about inclusion/exclusion I try to keep in mind an audience which includes both the countries of the North and the South. This choice of imagined surveillance is a reminder of supranational exclusionary forces and a need to be explicit about the context of my work. It involves adopting a comparative perspective, and I suggest that this is the paradigmatic discourse within social science, challenging us to reflect on our assumptions and parochial concepts. It demands that we move between vantage points, so that the strange is made familiar and the familiar made strange. It requires a recognition of the way academic exchange involves people at the apex of one set of cultural formations reaching out to those at another, within or between countries. However, a belief in a shared global academic discourse seduces many into thinking that they do not need to make this effort. What is produced in such a state of mind is a linguistic fog in which language becomes detached from the contexts which hold its meanings.

Engaging critique and complexity

In the following sections I take you on a brief and idiosyncratic tour of 'inclusion/exclusion' policy and debate in England in an attempt to capture the complexity of the issues and the mess we get ourselves into if we follow the restricted vision of 'inclusion' and 'exclusion' within official policy. I move between broader and narrower perspectives using a series of contrasting cameos.

In the next section I examine the muddle of debate about inclusion by looking into two cases of 'clear blue water'. The first reflects the joust between Conservative and Labour party politicians, over the virtues of selection by attainment for different types of secondary school at aged eleven. In 1997 the Conservative Prime Minister, John Major, described the advocacy of Grammar schools for high achievers in the last Bill considered by Parliament before his election defeat, as an attempt to put *'clear blue water'* between the education policies of his party and those of the opposition led by Tony Blair. I compare this argument over grammar schools with the attempt to place a similar distance between notions of 'inclusion' and 'integration'. In juxtaposing the two distinctions I ask whether the motives for making either of them are clear and whether there are parallels between them. In both cases, the water that I see has a cloudy, murky quality typical of the waters surrounding and dissecting England.

I then look at inclusion and exclusion as defined within government policies which set the discussion of inclusion on the sidelines of education. I point out their fragmentation and suggest that this is exacerbated by the viewing of difficulties in education as arising from the 'special educational needs' of learners. I look in particular at the proposals to revise (and keep the same) the Code of Practice on the Identification and Assessment of Children with Special Educational Needs (DfE 1994, DfEE 1999a). A minimal revision is proposed that is meant to make the document encourage greater 'inclusion'. Yet making the Code of Practice reflect a coherent inclusive philosophy would require its transformation.

My final example illustrates the attempt of myself and colleagues to take control of our conceptualisation of inclusion policy and practice in a study called 'Inclusion in the City'. In it, we explore the balance between inclusionary and exclusionary forces acting on learners in 'Melder'. I provide extracts from a case study where I have examined selection for religious denomination schools from their neighbourhoods. I consider the likely growth of Islamic Education and reactions to it, and ask with what forms of inclusion the continuation and growth of religious denomination schools is compatible.

I end the chapter by reiterating that inclusion/exclusion policy and discussion must be moved into the heart of education policy if it is to help to reveal rather than paper over the contradictions of an education system that claims to serve all learners while continuing to marginalise large numbers of them.

Muddying the waters of inclusion/exclusion

I do not think it is too difficult to persuade others, who do not have a vested interest in keeping it within the confines of 'special needs education', that inclusion/exclusion is about the shape of all aspects of education and social policy. Yet it is a peculiar feature of discussions of inclusion in England, as elsewhere, that such connections are rarely pursued. The study of the categorisation and special educational response to disabled learners and others seen as 'having special educational needs' is only part of the examination of selective processes in education, which also encompass divisions and discrimination related to attainment, presumed ability, age, gender, religion, class, ethnicity and wealth.

The debate about selection in education has most commonly been concerned with selection for an especially valued education in Grammar schools, by high attainment, at age eleven, with proponents and opponents of such a split, traditionally thought to divide along party political lines. The avoidance of the link between inclusion and selection by attainment, for example, has been partly tactical, with a desire for clarity giving way to political expediency. Under a Conservative regime, those concerned with pushing for greater inclusion of 'some' marginalised learners did not want to alienate the government by linking their advocacy to the red rag of comprehensive community education. And under a Labour government there may be a reluctance to point out too strongly the contradiction between the advocacy of inclusion in some policies in the context of an education system where the competitive, selective, pressures between schools exert a strong exclusionary force. I regard such contortions as self-defeating. However, a brief recent history of attitudes to such selection reveals a more complex story. I contrast this story, well known in English education as a site of political manoeuvring, with a distinction between 'integration' and 'inclusion' which is now so widely repeated that it has taken on a ritual quality. No paper or conference presentation about inclusion/exclusion seems quite complete without it. Could convoluted motives underlie the maintenance of such a distinction too?

Naturalising selection?

There have always been major departures from the neat party political divisions between the supporters and opponents of comprehensive secondary education. The division of schools into grammar for the élite, technical schools for those expected to enter skilled trades (though very few were actually established) and secondary modern schools for the rest, devised by a Conservative majority in the wartime coalition government was initially promoted by the 1945 post-war Labour government. It only began to be dismantled in the mid-1960s initially by a Labour government and then most rapidly by a conservative government in which Margaret Thatcher was Secretary of State for Education. (For a fuller account see Benn and Chitty 1996, Booth, Ainscow and Dyson 1998, Simon 1991). The New Right, Conservative government of 1979, inherited a secondary education system that was largely comprehensive. It recognised the electoral unpopularity of openly reverting to a selective system but there was a new determination to undo the socialist and communitarian taints of this system. The government set about dismantling it from within. Selection by attainment within secondary and upper primary school subjects was strongly encouraged. Local education policies concerned about reducing inequality of regard in the curriculum because of differences of gender, and particularly sexual orientation and ethnicity, were ridiculed as 'loony left'.

The success of the undermining of the comprehensive ideal can be judged by the performance of the shadow secretary of state for education, Jack Straw, who at a focus group at which I was present in the mid-1980s was asked why the Labour Party did not defend multicultural comprehensive education against the attacks from the Conservative Party. His reply was that 'there are no votes in it'. It became a very rare school after this period which would proclaim its comprehensive nature in the name at the school gates.

Selection between schools was effectively reintroduced under the banner of parental choice which enabled schools to select learners on the basis of their parental background. Schools competed against each other for positions on league tables of examination results and the middle class parents most likely to play the system. The shift to comprehensive schools had never been complete, with, for example, the second most populous city, Birmingham, retaining a grammar school system. Under the new regime such schools appeared to be beacons of high achievement. Popular schools were allowed to expand and less popular schools withered. This added to the difficulties of inner city areas which suffered most school closures and the consequent stress on their social fabric. In some cities three rings of schools became discernible, those in the inner ring were closing, in the next schools felt threatened with closure and in the commuter villages they thrived to the extent of bussing out learners from the city. When an inner city school closed other schools might compete *not* to take the students. A teacher in an outer ring school summarised what was happening to schools in his area by the latter part of the 1990s as government education policies were added to housing divided along class lines:

> 'I think the problem is in our society. Any school is going to be distorted. It is not going to be genuinely comprehensive because we have a class system in our society. I don't believe in bussing in that situation. I think people should be going to the local school. [But] every morning a bus is going to come outside of this school, two minutes down the road. I do not think that is acceptable. It becomes a self-perpetuating thing as well. Another 50 or 60 students coming in a year, who were getting grade Cs [at the 16+ examinations] could completely transform the school. That bus coming here rather than going to [Named School in commuter village] would have a significant impact ...
>
> Essentially, in this area, I think that this will become the secondary modern school, the other will become the secondary modern/technical

school and [the schools in the commuter villages] will be the grammar schools even though they are within the same so-called comprehensive system. I don't ever believe that the government's proposals were about partnership with parents. When there are 1,000 places and 1,200 apply, the power is with the head teacher, not the parent.'

Another teacher at the same school recorded the dilemma she and her family faced with a system that could suddenly make a school in their area struggle for survival and drew a parallel with her withdrawal from a health service decreasingly funded to cope with the demands upon it:

'I do not believe in selection. I don't. I did not send my children to selective schools. They went to the state school, but the situation being as it is, I think I may be supporting my grandchildren to a selective school not because I approve of it any more than I approve of private medicine but I am now using private medicine ... Politically I don't agree with selection and I don't believe in private medicine ... You just have to see how it works and you do the best for your own family under the present circumstances.'

These interviews took place just after a prominent member of the then Labour Opposition had elected to send her child out of her district to a grammar school and many of the teachers felt betrayed by this action as did many members of the Labour Party. A boundary between New and Old Labour began to be drawn around such issues. One Labour MP, Jeremy Corbyn, reported that his marriage had begun to founder because his wife wanted to send their son to a selective school outside of the inner London Borough of Islington, where he lived. The Labour leader, soon to be Prime Minister, Tony Blair, and his wife, lived in the same borough, but they agreed on sending their child to a high-status and effectively selective Catholic school in another part of London. It was part of the Oratory Foundation where the priests retained the conservative tradition of the Latin Mass which they delivered with their backs to the congregation, an image which matched the feelings in the hearts of many within the Labour Party.

Teachers, in two of the studies in which I am currently engaged, have described the continuing process of ethnic flight where when one ethnic group predominates above a certain level in a school then other groups move to different schools thus making the schools more ethnically homogeneous than the surrounding areas until rehousing choices catch up (Halstead 1988). In areas like Islington, home to the Blairs and the Corbyns, the same applies to class divisions. Hutton (1995) and Giddens (1999) both point out the stress on the education system of the self-exclusion from state services of the wealthy.

When the Labour Party came to power in 1997 there was little change of direction from the Conservative reforms of education. Mixed attainment teaching, in secondary schools and in the last stages of primary schools, continued to be seen as a major barrier to learner progress. This was at a time when the mixed attainment grouping throughout the first three years of secondary schools was already very rare (Benn and Chitty 1996). Bottom 'sets' were made up, largely, of boys thought to be difficult in behaviour who also were categorised as having special needs. The prevailing orthodoxy, overruled the legal requirement within the 1996 Education Act that such categorised students should be educated alongside students not so categorised.

A visitor from South Africa, witnessing the extent of grouping by attainment within English secondary schools, was horrified by such a degree of exclusion within the system. However, she did not acknowledge the exclusionary pressures exerted by the grade system in South Africa. The idea that only those students who achieve the grade should advance to the next class is so deeply ingrained in the system that despite its prohibition within the educational reforms in South Africa the practice is still widely retained. This is a striking divergence between central policy and local practice, though such adaptation of central policy is also common in England. Thus an inner-city school, described by one learner as, 'a good school whoever you are: black, white, disabled, non-disabled', prides itself on its mixed attainment teaching for all its learners aged 11 to 16 years. The head teacher deliberately trained as a school inspector in order to ensure that she knew the inspection ropes. Her school was given a glowing report.

In 1999 Islington was named by the government as an area in which standards of education were unacceptable and some of its services were to be taken over by other Education administrations and private companies (*TES*, 14 May 1999, p. 1). The government response to such failings is to try to prop up schools and areas in difficulty with a whole range of new policies, as illustrated by the document *Excellence in Cities* (DfEE 1999c). Some of the thinking within this document shows a new recognition by government of the problems faced by schools in the most economically disadvantaged areas of the inner cities and outer city social housing estates, though some of the solutions, like 'more setting' seem less well considered. Yet, whatever the failings of the administration in a district like Islington the emergence of failing areas, like failing schools, could be predicted solely on the basis of government policies encouraging the extinction of the most vulnerable.

In June 1999, however, Tony Blair, presiding over a government which had fervently embraced the selective education policies of the previous regime, gave a speech to the National Association of Head Teachers in which he attacked selection for secondary education:

> People don't want to go back to a system which divides 11 year olds into successes and failures ... I personally meet people for whom

rejection at 11 was the most devastating thing that happened to them as children and stayed with them for the rest of their lives. (*Daily Mail*, 3 June 1999, p. 1)

This rhetoric appears disconnected from a knowledge of the effects of government education policies. A Conservative spokesman responded by arguing for the merits of grammar schools. He might have claimed that, because of policies bequeathed to the Labour government, the argument had already been won.

Dividing and ruling the discourses of 'integration' and 'inclusion'

In this book Jenny Corbett and Roger Slee draw a customary distinction between 'integration' and 'inclusion'. They see 'integration' as 'inherently assimilationist' requiring learners to fit into a uni-cultural, 'mono-dimensional' mainstream. 'Inclusion' on the other hand requires a transformation of education, a challenge to 'existing hierarchies of status and privilege'. Felicity Armstrong, Brigitte Belmont and Aliette Verillon, in their chapter, see integration and inclusion in the context of the French education system as 'two opposing political goals' (see also Sebba 1997, Sebba and Ainscow 1996). In the United States the word 'mainstreaming' is substituted for 'integration'. For example, Ware (1998a) describes 'mainstreaming' as the instruction of students with disabilities outside of 'the regular class' whereas inclusion involves the presumption of belonging to a regular class in the neighbourhood school. I believe that the common attempts to contrast 'mainstreaming' or 'integration' as assimilation with 'inclusion' as educational transformation, amount to the use of 'a formula', that serves a number of purposes, but makes thinking about the issues more difficult.

Now, a distinction between assimilationist and transformative views of the inclusion of marginalised people is clearly important. I drew just such a distinction in examining conceptions of *integration* (Booth 1988). So, perhaps my wish to hold back the tide of language use may appear trivial or obstructive. I have encountered a strong reaction to my challenge of the 'formula' from a colleague; that I was being arrogant in criticising a distinction adopted by disabled people. He argued that disabled people had decided to use the terms in that way, that the formulation represents an important and easily assimilable distinction which can be translated into practice readily. Others have reiterated this last point, that they use the distinction in teaching to convey important differences in practice (Florian 1999). Yet I think the formulation of the distinction involves a misunderstanding of the purpose of definitions, a misinterpretation of practice and, in some cases, an incomplete analysis of the contents of a transformative inclusion agenda.

Definitions can be divided, usefully, into those that are descriptive and record the way words are used and those that are prescriptive and suggest that a particular use is adopted. My definitions of inclusion/exclusion are prescriptive. I claim that others do *not* use the concepts in the way I do. The commonly asserted difference between 'integration' and 'inclusion' does not represent the use of either word. A brief examination of the literature shows that integration and mainstreaming were, and inclusion is, used in a variety of ways (for example see Chapter 5 of this book, Booth 1983, 1988, Booth and Ainscow 1998a, Dunn 1968, Hegarty and Pocklington 1981, Hegarty 1993, and Ware 1998a). The definition cannot be about the use of both words. Yet if it is meant as a prescription it is an odd one, since 'integration' has largely been superseded by inclusion. We are recommended to think that it *was* used in a particular way. Perhaps a revision of history provides a third form of definition.

Now, often 'integration' *was* used to refer to practice which at best provided support in an unreconstructed mainstream and at worst provided presence with little support and it is important to move on from such practice. However, frequently, the advocacy of integration was opposed vehemently, which hardly squares with a process that did not challenge the status quo. It provoked all the forms of condemnation documented in relation to the advocacy of inclusion in the States by Ellen Branlinger (1996). For any proposal for the transformation of schools and the education system is likely to meet with resistance. Where 'integration' or 'inclusion' are perceived to be linked with a political project involving a reduction in all forms of discrimination in society including inequities in the distribution of wealth and status the opposition will be colossal. The way that 'integration', 'mainstreaming' or 'inclusion' are used, then, commonly falls far short of the transformative.

'Inclusion' has an unprecedented popularity within central government policy documents in England, which should come as a surprise to those who see it as having an intrinsically radical meaning. For it is applied in such a way as to imply very little change. As I shall discuss further in the next section, it is not used to inform, let alone transform general education policy, but is confined, largely, to documents about categorised learners or as 'social inclusion' in relation to issues of truancy and indiscipline (DfEE 1998, 1999b). In *Meeting Special Educational Needs; a programme of action* (DfEE 1998), 'inclusion' is said to be 'the keystone of policy' (p. 8). Inclusion is seen narrowly as 'providing as far as possible for children's special educational needs within mainstream schools' (p. 8). Further it is envisaged that special schools will continue to 'play a vital role as part of an inclusive local education system' (p. 23). The Tomlinson report, *Inclusive Learning*, is seen by many as establishing inclusion at the centre of futher education policies. Inclusion in this report is defined as 'matching the resources we have to the learning styles and educational needs of the students' (Tomlinson 1997, p. 193). It carries no implications for shared participation with peers, even to the extent of presence in the same college, and is contrasted in this respect with *integration* which is seen to require shared learning experiences. In England, at end of the 1990s, it seems that 'inclusion' is used by many to define an agenda more distant from the transformative than the way 'integration' was often used and that the advocacy of inclusion meets with more ready acceptance than did the proposals for integration in previous decades.

There are definite advantages to replacing the term 'integration' with 'inclusion'. Foremost among them is the link this encourages between the processes of inclusion and the reduction of exclusion both within and beyond the mainstream. But there are disadvantages. Inclusion has gained global currency, and although there is no going back on its adoption, there is a danger that people believe that shared meanings can be achieved without cultural contextualisation. However, integration, besides being used to define a strictly educational project, carried the sense of putting things together, both learners and systems, and the latter idea, one might argue, is a more powerful suggestion of change than is often seen to be implied by inclusion.

There are aspects of the definition of inclusion in the formula that frequently fall short of the transformative. The view of inclusion within it, generally retains the common concern of those who supported 'integration' with some learners rather than all learners. It thus fits neatly with the marginalisation of inclusion by government outside of mainstream education policy in a discourse which links the education of disabled learners with the medical model of difficulties in learning, contained in policies on 'special educational needs'. I argue that a transformative agenda is concerned with overcoming barriers to learning of all students who experience excluding pressures at all levels of the system.

In addition, the formula involves seeing 'integration' and 'inclusion' as representing two states; presence in, and full participation within, the mainstream, respectively. Yet I have suggested that both integration and inclusion should be seen to involve unending processes of transformation. The terms 'access' and 'participation' do a better job of marking the distinction between 'arriving at the station' and 'getting on the train'[1], than 'integration' and 'inclusion'.

The responsiveness of systems to people, seen to be the pre-eminent feature of inclusion by some, is only part of what makes up a transformative inclusion agenda as Corbett and Slee recognise. Inclusion as transformation involves seeing difference within education as an aspect of reality to be welcomed and celebrated and as a key resource for learning rather than a source of difficulty. It recognises the tyranny of views of normality as homogeneity and sees normality as constituted only by difference. It starts from an assumption of difference in groups of learners and involves a pedagogy for diversity.

A transformative inclusion agenda also involves a shift away from professional control over education to the assertion of learner rights and entitlements. It is as concerned with issues relevant to countries of the South as the North. The fragmentation of policies in relation to general education, special needs education, and inclusive education is wasteful and obstructive in relation to countries of the North but does even greater harm in countries of the South (see UNESCO 1998).

How do we account for the popularity of the distinction between 'integration' and 'inclusion'? It simplifies ideas and makes them readily assimilable and this may be attractive in the short term although in the longer term it makes clear thought more difficult. It has a sound bite quality which fits the spirit of the times. It suggests a break in thinking between new views and the traditionalists and thus marks out its users as thoroughly modern thinkers, can be seen as a bid for control over the discourse and avoids grappling with a more complex messy history of political struggles over inclusion and exclusion which match those over selection by attainment within education. However, I suggest that it arises primarily because of a failure of the 'inclusion/exclusion' debate to break free from the marginalised position allocated to it within government policy documents. The critique of 'integration' in 'the formula' relates to the way that *official* 'integration' policies were conceptualised and the practices in schools that they encouraged. This conceptualisation remains virtually unchanged despite a switch to the term 'inclusion'. It is to a brief critique of this official view that I now turn.

Inclusion from the sidelines

The exclusionary pressures within the education system, and the widening gap in wealth between the richest and poorest communities should provide contexts for framing government policies on inclusion and exclusion. With a brief respite in the mid-1990s, these disparities have increased considerably over two decades (Howarth et al. 1998). This is acknowledged, apparently, by the government's establishment of the Social Exclusion Unit within the Cabinet Office. However, as I have argued, when translated into education the links with broader social and educational policies are lost, and the notion of inclusion becomes restricted. Policies that originate within the Social Exclusion Unit are translated into education as 'social inclusion' policies and are given a narrower focus.

There are a plethora of documents which state that they contain an inclusionary intent. In addition to those already mentioned on social exclusion and social inclusion. *Meeting Special Educational Needs: A programme of action* (DfEE 1998) was preceded by a Green Paper *Excellence For All Children: Meeting Special Educational Needs* (DfEE

1997b) in which inclusion was the 'big idea'. A semi-autonomous body called the Teacher Training Agency, with increasing control over initial teacher education, head-ship education and in-service education for teachers, produced guidelines for 'special educational needs coordinators' and a consultation on guidelines for 'specialist teachers' which also referred to inclusion (TTA 1998a and b). There were so many objections to the exclusionary model underlying the 'training' of a wide range of specialists for categorised groups that a revised version of the latter document has not reappeared.

The discussion of one document appears to be carried out in isolation from the discussion of others. No links are made between the exclusion of disabled people or children and young people categorised as having 'special educational needs' and *social* inclusion/exclusion largely seen to concern learner behaviour. All of these are conceived separately from policies about learners whose home language is different from the language of instruction.

The 'social inclusion division' in the Department for Education and Employment is a separate sub-department from the 'special educational needs' division. When I rang the 'Special Needs Division' mistakenly thinking that they could send me the document on 'social inclusion', the people working there had never heard of the 'School Inclusion Division'. I later discovered they all work on the same corridor.

Some of the suggestions in recent documents represent a development in government thinking. The document on 'social inclusion' links truancy and 'school' or 'disciplinary' exclusion and encourages centres of learning to see reluctant attendance as a form of exclusion (DfEE 1999b). Further it highlights the barriers to learning and participation experienced by learners in 'families under stress', children looked after by the state, ethnic minority learners, travellers, learners who have responsibility for the care of other family members and those moving between institutions. Such a broad examination of groups vulnerable to exclusion can be used as a starting point to link all learners who experience barriers to learning, within a common policy framework.

However, in responding to government policy it is tempting to overplay the progress that is made. The 'programme of action' says that the government 'will encourage all schools to develop an inclusive ethos, for example by involving all staff in training activities to promote a greater understanding of inclusion' (DfEE 1998, p. 25). The report argues that 'an increasing number of schools are showing that an inclusive approach can reinforce a commitment to higher standards of achievement for all children' (p. 23). They suggest that schools less able to respond to learners who experience difficulties must learn from others: 'we will work and provide funding ... to ensure that the high quality provision for children with complex needs which some mainstream schools are already making, is available much more widely ... It is not good enough simply to say that local mainstream schools have not previously included a child with these needs' (pp. 23–4). The emphasis on precedent can be a powerful new pressure for increasing inclusion since practice varies so widely from one local area to another. Such extracts give the impression that policy *across the education system* is to be pushed to increase inclusion and participation and reduce exclusion until one examines the narrowness of the view of inclusion, support in it for the maintenance of special schools and its lack of relationship to education policies *as a whole*.

It is difficult to provide an effective critique to a fragmented set of policies. In responding to draft documents we are not expected to question the assumptions within which they are framed. Yet, it is important for critique to engage with the framing ideologies of government policies if we are to take control of our own practice.

Coded exclusion

Responses to government policies have to be strategic. They must recognise what is already in place within the education system and require a careful analysis of the way a proposed set of changes will take the system nearer to a desired goal. Such attempts have to be understood within the detail of the policies and distributions of power between central, local government, schools, governors and teacher unions at a particular historical juncture in England.

The Code of Practice, on the Identification and Assessment of Children with Special Educational Needs, implemented from September 1994 exerts considerable power in shaping and limiting inclusion policy and practice in schools. The consultation document on revisions to this Code of Practice which suggests that it be made consistent with 'a more inclusive approach', anticipates that it will be subject to only minor change. Yet it remains locked into a response to difficulties in learning experienced by children and young people which predates the Warnock Report of 1978 (DES 1978). In it, difficulties in learning are attributed to the 'special educational needs' of learners which are seen as deficiencies of individuals. There is the occasional acknowledgement of a different view. For example, para 2.19 suggests that 'schools should not automatically assume that children's learning difficulties always result solely or even mainly from problems within the child'; however, a view that problems are to be attributed to the deficiencies of individual learners and require remediation targeted at individuals is the overwhelmingly predominant view. It is the child rather than a concern about the teaching and learning environment which is officially 'registered' within a school. This is reinforced in the suggestion within the consultation document that an individual plan for learners whose education causes concern should focus on three or four short-term targets *'for the child'* (DfEE

1999a). The approach to the 'statementing process', which singles out for assessment learners who are seen to experience protracted difficulties requiring additional support, similarly directs attention at child deficits. It is this formal categorisation process that determines the character of the Code, taking up three quarters of its pages.

I have proposed that the pressure on pushing learners through the statementing process in order to gain 'additional resources' for a school, would be considerably reduced by the careful formulation of an entitlement *to support* for all learners in schools who need it. A definition of entitlement to support would require the specification of maximum class sizes throughout the system and staff/learner ratios for the allocation of support teachers and assistants, related to the economic and social context of the area. At present 'learning support' is commonly conceived in terms of one 'special needs coordinator' in a school irrespective of its size, and in addition, whoever else is allocated to the school on the basis of individual 'statements of special educational needs'. An effective learning support strategy cannot be constructed in this way.

It is of interest, culturally, but hardly conducive to inclusion that, at the end of the twentieth century, the Code encourages a particular group of teachers to self-categorise themselves as 'SENCOs', using a discriminatory label that they carry around like a bell summoning the 'dull and backward' to come forward and be identified. The concepts used for understanding educational difficulties, within the Code, have remained unchanged for more than 25 years. Yet an emphasis on seeing educational difficulties as due to the 'special educational needs' of learners is itself a barrier to inclusion. It discourages the reflection on changes in organisation, curricula and teaching approaches which might contribute most to increasing the quality and extent of participation of learners within local centres of learning.

I argue that the notion of 'barriers to learning and participation', a version of which has been adopted for the framework of legislation in South Africa (NCSNET 1997) and taken up within discussion documents in UNESCO (UNESCO 1998) can productively replace the term 'special educational needs'. Barriers to learning and participation can occur at all levels of the system. Within classrooms the analysis of the barriers to learning and participation always involves an exploration of the teaching and learning environment. The process of overcoming or minimising barriers to learning and participation requires the identification of the human resources, in staff, learners, parents and other members of the community, as well as the material resources that can bemobilised, at all points in the system, to support inclusion.

This move away from the identification of the barriers to progress of learners with their 'special educational needs' is compatible with Susan Hart's important work on 'innovative thinking' which she suggests should be brought to play when the learning of a student is a cause for concern (Hart

1996). She has worked with teachers to apply her model to learners who have English as an additional language, thus bringng the educational response to such learners and others whose learning is causing concern within a single framework (LcaS 1999). Working with the concepts of barriers to learning and participation, the identification and mobilising of resources to support inclusion and participation and developments in 'innovative thinking', provide more powerful ways to encourage learner and school improvement than the concepts of 'children with special educational needs' and 'special educational provision'. The avoidance of this discriminatory language within the Code would permit the formulation of a single policy document, uniting all aspects of support for learner diversity. It would be about the development of inclusive cultures, policies and practices in schools, and the support of all learners within them.

Taking control of inclusion in the city

In my final example I look at the way colleagues and I have attempted to set our own agenda for exploring inclusion/exclusion in the city of Melder. Inclusion is related, within Melder, to strategies for improving schools so that they become more responsive to the diversity of their learners. But the predominant view of inclusion held by local authority officers in Melder is couched in the terms set out in national policy documents. We are contrasting an exploration of the Local Authority 'inclusion' policies with examining broader concerns, central to our understanding of school communities and what it means to be included in them. A colleague is investigating the implications of high learner mobility on the nature of school communities and the extent to which housing policies can and should reduce such mobility. A further case study will examine selection by attainment within and between schools, another selection by gender. We are looking at the relationship between support structures and practice for learners who have English as an additional language and learning support for learners categorised as having 'special educational needs'. Others look at ways of assessing inclusionary and exclusionary pressures within school cultures and at the possibilities for creating 'inclusive' communities within further education colleges.

Hierarchies of faith in the city?

In my first case study for the project I have looked at the relationship between religious denomination schools and their communities, focusing on a Catholic Primary School, a Church of England Secondary School and an Islamic Primary School which was one of the first such schools to receive state funding. I have asked with what forms of inclusion selection by religion is compatible.

Denominational schools make up a third of all schools in England, have a very significant effect on the relationship between schools and their communities, the possibilities for learners attending their neighbourhood school, the nature of their experience when they are there and the prospects for teachers of different faiths or no faith. Almost all religious denomination schools in England are voluntary aided or voluntary controlled. The significant difference being that the former, where the religious authorities make a 15 per cent contribution to building capital and repair, have greater control over the religious education curriculum, admissions and staffing. Most Church of England schools are voluntary controlled (about 60 per cent) whereas all Catholic schools are voluntary aided.

In the study, I encountered various forms of 'a dilemma' for my informants between a school serving a community of the faithful and responding to its surrounding communities. I found a similar variation in the way this dilemma might be resolved from informants connected to either Catholic or Church of England schools. The dilemma was spelled out for me by both the Church of England Diocesan Director of Education, and the Executive Secretary of the Catholic Diocesan Schools Commission. As expressed by the former:

> 'Within any of our schools we would want to provide opportunities for the development of the C of E faith. This is not indoctrination, shoving it down someone's throat but within a C of E school there should be an opportunity for any pupil to grow in Christian faith if they so wish.
> We have a *dilemma* in the C of E because our trustees talk about schools for the *local* community ... we would hope that the parishes and schools would be welcoming to all faiths and have a role as the *established* faith to help bind communities together. If we fear anything we fear segregation of communities which could happen.'

There is ambivalence here towards learners who are not of the faith and in addition to a order of merit in relation to those that embrace a faith and have no faith. There is also an assertion of a hierarchy of faiths through the position of the Church of England as the Established religion.

The Catholic Executive Secretary of the Diocesan Schools Commission, indicated, too, how Catholic schools were 'basically there for Catholic children' but pointed out how circumstances could affect the composition of the schools:

> 'In the early 70s in part of [Melder] where the communities were changing and the immigrants were coming in and our numbers were going down, the Archbishop of the time ... said if you've got room to

fit some of the Afro-Caribbean or the Asian population in, because ...
it's contrary to what Catholic schools are all about to be paragons of
white faces in the community ...

So like St [name of church] is right in the middle of the Asian
community in [Melder]. They're half and half. The governors guided
by the Diocese have made that decision. It's a Catholic school, run on
Catholic principles. The staff are Catholic, RE is all Catholic. The
community actually love it and are clamouring to get in. The governors
have made the decision that they are quite happy to have quite a high
percentage of Afro-Caribbean and Asian pupils around the place.'

There is a suggestion that there was a pragmatic modification of
philosophy in the schools, to the pressures of history. And in practice, as
reported to me by several teachers, a concern to be at the heart of the
neighbourhood often followed the change in the nature of the surrounding
community so that learners committed to the designated religion of the school
were in short supply for both Catholic and Church of England schools.

In the Catholic Primary School I visited, there was a quota of 10 per cent
non-Catholics. The school gave priority to practising Catholics and only took
in non-Catholics to make up the numbers. However, changes in the area were
reflected in the very different composition of the non-denominational
nursery attached to the school. The head was unsure whether the Trustees of
the school would be willing to change the selection criteria and thought the
school might be threatened with closure within a few years. He had decided
to accept a post at another Catholic school with a more liberal admissions
policy.

Within the Church of England Secondary School 60 per cent of the
students had a Muslim background, although in theory the school still gave
priority to Church of England students. However, a shift in the philosophy of
the school had been so thoroughly adopted that the head felt that if the school
became more popular with Christian students they might have to change the
admission criteria and impose a quota on them so as not to unbalance the
relationship with the local community. Yet this was already unbalanced
because boys outnumbered girls in a ratio of two to one partly as a result of
Muslim parents avoiding sending their daughters to a mixed sex school. The
head was concerned at the way the imbalance and the relatively poor
attainments of boys affected the position of the school in league tables of
examination results.

The development of Islamic schools

The Islamic school was set up in response to a feeling of some Muslim
teachers and many members of the Islamic community that Muslim children
did not receive an education which respected their Muslim identity. They

were concerned about representation on governing bodies, the nature of the curriculum, the availability of single sex schools particularly for girls, and the lack of attention to prohibitions on exposure of the body in PE for both boys and girls. Established in a predominantly Muslim area, it would be many years before the school would have to face changes in the ethnic composition of the surrounding community, and a consequent challenge to the religious character of the school since it had a waiting list of 1,500 students.

Given this demand for Islamic schools their numbers are likely to rise considerably. A Muslim teacher in another Authority, which as yet has no state funded Islamic schools, explained how the vast majority of Muslim teachers in the Authority would prefer to teach in an Islamic school and to send their children to one:

> 'I am sure if you ask the right questions then you will get pretty much the same kind of answers from I would say more than 90 per cent of the Muslim staff.'

The compatibility of religious denomination schools and inclusion

The prospect of the growth of Islamic schools was concentrating the minds of others within the communities of Melder. A Sikh informant claimed that his community were also thinking about separate schooling:

> 'If there is a tendency in the country as a whole that every faith has its own schools then you have to have for your survival ... If the trend continues; the Muslims have their schools, the Jews have their own schools, Christians have their schools, then at some point we have to say: "Yes we will have our own schools".'

Both the Catholic and Church of England authorities acknowledged the justice of the Muslim argument not to face discrimination in the funding of religious denomination schools. And in the case of the head of the Church of England Secondary School, she felt that her logic demanded an end to all such schools:

> If the existence of my school and others like it means that we're going to have more and more groups setting up their own schools then *if the Catholics would go along with it* ... personally, I would get rid of Church of England schools now. It's not a typical view ... but I feel so strongly that the only way forward is to educate children together which we do here ... I think that gives an opportunity for increased understanding.

But the penalty for us being here is going to be more and more initially Islamic schools. I suspect that will only be the beginning. I think we might get pressure from Hindus next ... and for various sections of the Christian community for different types of schools. We could end up with a situation where more and more children go to segregated schools where they don't meet the general run of the population. I think that's really bad for the pupils and I feel very strongly about it ... There's going to be greater and greater division ...'

This extract from the study of religious denomination schooling in the city of Melder provides a flavour of the way religion relates to issues of inclusion within schools and how this is being played out in England at the end of the century. In the medium term there are likely to be more Islamic schools and in the short term there will be a continuing demand for single sex education particularly for girls. Yet at the same time the discriminatory pressures on Muslims in non-denominational schools should not be compounded by an exclusionary refusal to allow Islamic schools to be funded on the same bases as other denominational schools.

Concluding remarks

In this chapter I have tried to portray some of the complexities of understanding inclusion policy and practice within England and by implication within any country. I have suggested that, in discussing inclusion/exclusion, we need to take on board all forms of selection within education. I have pointed out that inclusion/exclusion does not lie at the heart of gove.nment education policies and that even within the margina' position given to it by government, policies remain fragmented. This official version of inclusion policy interferes with the sensible articulation of the inclusion project and its translation into practice.

I have noted the unprecedented popularity of 'inclusion' in government documents. This may arise for a mixture of reasons. It suits government rhetoric, particularly one that traditionally aligned itself with the economically vulnerable sections of society, to encourage its traditional supporters by using the rhetoric of inclusion and the reduction of 'social exclusion', while pursuing policies that will do little to reduce inequalities. But there is also a positive trend discernible on the ground, where groups of teachers up and down the country seem eager to advocate inclusion. They appear to welcome a rallying point from which to counter the harshness of competitive education policies which place little value on the sustenance of community.

The absence of a recognition of the social consequences of contemporary education policies has allowed the creation of a divisive approach to raising achievement in schools that may take some years to be played out. Discussions of inclusion/exclusion can help to reveal the contradictions in such policies if debate is freed from its inherited connection with 'special needs education', which impedes the process of transforming schools so that they celebrate and encourage the full participation of all learners in their communities.

Note

1. This distinction comes from David Ruebain's comments on the Disability Discrimination Act of 1995 which literally required railway stations to be accessible but not public transport.

Chapter 7

Inclusion and choice: mutually exclusive principles in special educational needs?

Sheila Riddell

Introduction

The aim of this chapter is to explore the ways in which two key principles in the arena of special educational needs, choice and inclusion, have been used in very different ways within official policy and by those promoting change within the disability movement. The range of meanings embedded in these terms is not random, but rather reflects competing political goals. This chapter begins with an analysis of the discourses of inclusion and choice in national policy documents and the thinking of the disability movement. This is followed by an analysis of official statistics, which suggests that the tension between the two principles of inclusion and choice has produced a state of policy stasis, with patterns of placement of children with special educational needs being at variance with official rhetoric. Case study data from a research project conducted in the Department of Education, University of Stirling between 1992 and 1995 (Allan, Brown and Riddell 1995) are used to illustrate the ways in which the principles of choice and integration are experienced by parents of children with special educational needs and the young people themselves.

Before looking in more detail at the discourses surrounding choice and integration, let us consider briefly the theoretical framework informing this analysis. Fulcher (1989), reflecting on her experience of observing a review of special educational needs policy in Victoria, Australia, noted the way in which a range of discourses played a crucial role in establishing how policy was understood. She commented:

> I saw that how language is used matters. It was the instrument of power.
> (p. 4)

For example, to assert that 'integration had always been with us' (because some disabled children were placed in mainstream schools), was to suggest that there was no need to develop this policy any further. Other contenders maintained that, because many disabled children continued to spend part of their time in special units outside the mainstream classroom, integration could not be claimed to be taking place. What was needed, argued this group, was an entirely new understanding of the notion of integration. Fulcher maintained that such confusion did not arise because of misunderstandings over the nature of integration, but rather because language was used as a tactic in support of particular positions:

> How one talked about the issues revealed the politics of integration (to change or maintain the status quo?) and the nature of competing discourses. (p. 5)

In the same way as the term integration has been used to win support for very different and sometimes contradictory practices, so the idea of individual choice is generally assumed to be desirable, but may in practice have a wide range of meanings. As Stalker (1995) has noted, the notion of choice may be used to denote individual consumerism or collective empowerment, but there is a danger that the hegemony of individual consumerism may cause us to lose sight of wider ideas of group empowerment. In the following sections, I explore in rather more detail the way in which the notions of integration and choice have been used within official discourse and the work of the disability movement. Subsequently, I consider the way in which these discourses are reflected in current practice in the field of special educational needs as revealed in official statistics and the experiences of parents of children with special educational needs.

The Scottish policy context

In the following discussion, I have tried to maintain an awareness of the particular nature of the Scottish educational policy frame which differs markedly from both the US and UK contexts. In mainstream education, although there has been a process of marketisation, the system remains far more homogeneous than in England, with only a handful of schools opting out of local authority control and no selective or single sex schools within the state system (Lange Riddell 1999). Indeed, the new Scottish Parliament is committed to removing the possibility for schools to opt out of local authority control, but since so few schools have taken this route anyway the impact of this move will be negligible. There also remains a strong commitment to state education, although in the cities, many parents use parental choice to move their children into higher status state schools. In the area of special educational needs, raw statistics draw attention to marked differences north and south of the Border. For instance, if we compare 1997 data on the proportion of children with Records or Statements of Need, we find that in Scotland the highest use of mainstream is made by East Renfrewshire (61%),

North Ayrshire (57%) and Dumfries and Galloway (53%). In England, authorities making greatest use of mainstream are Newham (89%), Cornwall (89%) and Barnsley (87%). In the case of the three Scottish authorities and Cornwall, the high use of mainstream may be explained by their rural nature, since special schools would entail unacceptably long journeys for children. However, high levels of use of mainstream in Newham and Barnsley is driven by a commitment to inclusive education which is interpreted as placement in mainstream classes (Newham's commitment to inclusive education is described in an interview with the chair of Newham Council Education Committee in the journal *Special* (Griffiths 1999). In Scotland, inclusive education is beginning to feature rather more prominently in the policies adopted by the new authorities following local government reorganisation, for example Aberdeen City now has a commitment to inclusive education. This has been operationalised as the closure of special schools and the transfer of resources to special bases attached to mainstream. Every child in a special base has a place allocated to them in a mainstream school, but the time spent in the mainstream class may vary from 95 per cent to less than 5 per cent.

Despite the fact that authorities in Scotland have tended to shy away from identifying inclusion of children with special educational needs as a human rights issue, England and Scotland place about the same proportion of statemented/recorded pupils in mainstream schools (57 per cent in Scotland, 58 per cent in England). Scotland, then, seems to tread a middle course, tending to avoid an overt political commitment to inclusive education whilst making significant use of mainstream, often as a response to geographical factors. There are also marked contrasts between Scotland and the US (Lange and Riddell, forthcoming). In the US, charter schools and parental choice are seen by some special needs educators as the routes to more inclusive schooling, whilst in Scotland the prevailing view is that parental choice often works in opposition to inclusive principles since middle class flight from poorer schools means that some children become isolated in a depleted environment. In the commentary which follows, I attempt to describe the tensions between inclusion and choice which have, at times, led to the freezing of Scottish policy, compared with more dynamic environments elsewhere. Let us now consider the Warnock Report, regarded as playing a key role in shaping SEN policy in both England and Scotland in the 1970s.

The principles of inclusion and choice: official policy discourses

Policy documents of the 1970s

In the context of official discourse, the Warnock Report (DES 1978) provided a very strong endorsement of the principle of integration, referring to it as 'the central contemporary issue in special education'. Warnock argued:

> The principle of educating handicapped and non-handicapped children together, which is described as 'integration' in this country and 'mainstreaming' in the United States of America, and is recognised as a much wider movement of 'normalisation' in Scandinavia and Canada, is the particular expression of a widely held and still growing conviction that, as far as is humanly possible, handicapped people should share the opportunities for self-fulfilment enjoyed by other people. (para 7.1, p. 99)

Despite this support for integration, the ongoing role of special schools was affirmed as places of positive action through favourable resourcing arrangements.

With regard to the principle of choice, Warnock promoted the idea of partnership with parents in pursuit of the child's best interests. The report did not embrace fully the notion of parent as final arbiter of appropriate educational provision and was criticised by commentators such as Kirp (1982) for failing to endorse a rights approach but instead reinforcing the principle of professional discretion. Warnock, then, represented a cautious compromise, supporting parental wishes but failing to challenge professionals' ultimate control over decision making and championing the principle of integration whilst acknowledging the ongoing role of special schools.

A rather different balance was struck by a report from Scottish HMI (SED 1978) which argued for a much stronger commitment to the integration of children with learning difficulties into mainstream classes. Indeed, in the view of HMI, withdrawing children into segregated remedial classes tended to accentuate rather than alleviate their difficulties and distract attention from the central source of problems, the curriculum in mainstream schools. In this document, the principle of integration is seen as more important than the individual parent's right to choose their child's educational placement.

Yet another variation on the balance between the principles of integration and choice was struck by the 1980 Education (Scotland) Act (as amended). This legislation made no mention of educating children with special educational needs in mainstream classes, although provision for parental choice of school was extended to parents of children with special educational needs; it was assumed that parents who wished to do so could choose to have their children educated in a mainstream school. A range of caveats dealing with financial and administrative matters, however, imposed restrictions on the extent to which parents were able to exercise choices. Essentially, if it was felt that additional expense would be incurred by placing a child in a mainstream school, or this might be detrimental to the education of other children, then the placing request could be refused. Integration was not seen as an essential component of the system, but as an option if parents so wished and if the authority was able to resource it. If provision were to move in this direction, then parental choice had to be the engine of change in accordance with quasi-market principles (Bartlett *et al.* 1994).

Policy documents of the 1990s

By the 1990s, after more than a decade of Conservative government, the market and individual choice rather than collective welfare had become the established policy framework, evident in documents such as *The Parents' Charter for Scotland* (Scottish Office 1991) which promoted the following agenda:

- a sustained new programme for improving quality;
- an emphasis on choice, wherever possible between competing providers, as the best spur to quality improvement;
- the citizen's right to be told what service standards are and to be assured of action when service is unacceptable; and
- the need for public services to give value for money within a tax bill the nation can afford.

The language of equity and social justice was conspicuously absent from such statements. In their place was a conceptualisation of citizenship as consumption producing competition between providers which would raise standards and lead to greater value for money in the public sector.

In the area of special educational needs, the rhetoric of choice is noticeably more muted. The document *A Parents' Guide to Special Educational Needs* (SOED, 1993) indicated a number of caveats limiting the extent of choice. Among others, an education authority might refuse a placing request:

- if admitting your child would mean they would have to employ an additional teacher or spend a lot of money to adapt or otherwise extend the school;
- if your child's education would suffer from another change of school;
- if the kind of education provided in the school you want would not be suitable for the child;
- if your child's admission would affect the education of other children (because, say, he or she needs a very great deal of individual attention).

Nonetheless, in an updated version of *The Parents' Charter in Scotland* (1995) there was a reassurance that parents of children with special educational needs have the same right to choice of school as others and that the authority must undertake to cover costs incurred in placing a child in a school outwith the local authority boundary or where fees are incurred.

In the early 1990s, endorsement of the principle of integration as well as choice was evident (see SOED 1993, 1994). Decisions on placement tended to be framed in terms of meeting the needs of individual children, for instance, in the document *A Parents' Guide to Special Educational Needs*, integration is presented not as a governing principle but as a possible option which might be selected by individual parents on their children's behalf, almost as a lifestyle choice. The document *Effective Provision for Special Educational Needs* (SOED 1994) stated that placement in mainstream would be considered as the first option for a child with learning difficulties, but there was no consideration of the possible tension with the principle of choice. Confusion was reflected in local authority policy statements, as Labour-controlled authorities attempted to support integration whilst simultaneously endorsing the principle of choice. The message from some authorities seemed to be that parents were encouraged to choose, as long as this was in line with regional policy. One education authority document stated:

> A framework for integrated provision for pupils with special educational needs should be firmly based on the principles of choice and opportunity. It is essential that parents and young people involved should have the opportunity to exercise choice as to the location of placement. These principles necessitate the availability of provision in both special and mainstream schools. Parents, children and young people should be encouraged to exercise choice in the direction of mainstream education as far as possible. Equally, however, it should be recognised that parents have a right to have their child educated in a special school if they so wish.

As New Labour seeks to establish a distinctively different political philosophy from that of Old Labour and the Conservatives, such tensions are still in evidence. The wave of policy documents which has accompanied Labour's first year in office are reviewed below.

The New Labour agenda for special educational needs: communitarianism in action

The Labour Government, which came to power in May 1997, has attempted to pursue a middle way between a commitment to the market as the ultimate arbiter of public service provision and social democratic principles which are seen as placing too much emphasis on rights and not enough on responsibilities. In the words of Driver and Martell (1997):

> New Labour sell community as the hangover cure to the excess of conservative individualism. Community will create social cohesion out of the market culture of self-interest. And in Labour's dynamic market

economy, community will also be good for business, underpinning economic efficiency and individual opportunity. (p. 27)

In the White Paper *Excellence in Schools* (DfEE 1997a), we are told that education should be for the many, not for the few and market forces alone will not be sufficient to raise standards:

> We face new challenges at home and from international competitors, such as the Pacific Rim countries. They do not rely on market forces alone in education and neither should we. It is time to get to the heart of raising standards – improving the quality of teaching and learning. (p. 11)

In addition, the policy documents of the Labour government which have appeared thus far represent a significant break with the Conservative agenda by asserting that inclusive education reflects a moral imperative rather than simply being a response to the wishes of parents as consumers. However, acknowledging the paramount importance of the needs of individual children might be seen as the get-out clause ensuring the survival of special schools:

> Where pupils do have special educational needs there are strong educational, social and moral grounds for their education in mainstream schools. Our policy for schools will be consistent with our commitment to rights for disabled people more generally. But we must always put the needs of the child first, and for some children specialist, and perhaps residential, provision will be required, at least for a time. That is compatible with the principle of inclusive education. (DfEE 1997b, p. 34)

The English Green Paper on special educational needs, published in late 1997, makes clear that whilst actively promoting integration as the best option, there is a commitment to maintain the choices which parents already have:

> We want children with special educational needs to be educated in mainstream schools wherever possible. And we want to improve the way in which mainstream schools are able to meet special needs, so that most parents will want to choose mainstream schools for their child. But we will maintain parents' present right to express a preference for a special school place for their child, where they believe it necessary. And we shall ensure that, in opting for a mainstream school, parents of children with SEN have an increasing degree of real choice. (DfEE 1997b, p. 25)

In Scotland, a similar readjustment between market and social justice principles is also evident. A discussion paper entitled *Parents as Partners: A discussion paper* (SOEID 1998) readopts the language of partnership rather than consumerism, and emphasises influence through voice rather than exit (Hirschman 1970). Ways are sought to encourage parents to play a more active role in running schools through, for example, school boards rather than seeking to influence schools indirectly by taking their custom elsewhere if dissatisfied with the service on offer. A Green Paper on special educational needs in Scotland, published in May 1998, outlined the future direction for special educational needs provision in Scotland. A commitment is given to the development of a policy framework which does the following:

- places the child's educational needs at the centre of education policy and decision-making;
- ensures that special educational needs are routinely taken into account when framing and implementing education policies;
- develops the earliest practicable assessment of the educational needs of every child;
- promotes the earliest practicable intervention to tackle the needs identified;
- supports diversity of provision consistent with the diverse needs of the individual child;
- encourages and furthers the role of parents;
- places continuing and increasing priority on the development and training of staff working with children with special educational needs;
- ensures that every education authority prepares, publishes and makes readily available in consultation with relevant interests in this area a full policy on special educational needs. (SOEID 1998, p. 5)

'Selecting an appropriate placement' is listed as one of the ways in which parents may be involved in the education of their child. Other ways include: participating in assessment and review; suggesting effective approaches to teaching and learning; passing on to teachers relevant information from doctors and other professionals; offering advice to other parents and pupils in the school; supporting school activities; reinforcing new skills and learning at home and in the community. The general emphasis on 'working together' is much more in line with the Warnock idea of partnership than with the notion of parents exerting consumer power. There are also different nuances between the Scottish and English documents in their approach to inclusion. Whilst the English document makes clear that placement in mainstream is the preferred option, the Scottish counterpart is considerably more circumspect:

In recent years, there has been much discussion about the development of integration and inclusion for pupils with special educational needs. However there is no single universal answer to how these are achieved. An inclusive society must ensure that the potential of each individual is fully developed through education and that their attainment and achievement are developed and respected. It is on the realisation of this potential that inclusiveness depends; an inclusive society and education system will therefore strive to ensure that it creates the range of approaches and opportunities to ensure that this is brought about. (SOEID 1998, p. 4)

It appears that special educational needs policy, including tensions between choice and integration, may be worked out differently in England and Scotland and that these divergences may increase as the new Scottish Parliament becomes established, with education as one of its main areas of jurisdiction.

To summarise, the policy documents of the late 1970s supported integration, rather cautiously in the case of Warnock and more firmly in the case of the 1978 Progress Report of Scottish HMI. Legislation, on the other hand, affirmed parental choice (with a range of caveats) as the overriding principle, with an underlying assumption that many parents would favour integrated provision. By the early 1990s, government documents consistently reiterated the centrality of parental choice, although financial concerns introduced a number of constraints which meant that in practice parents of children with special educational needs had less freedom of choice than others. The Green Papers on special educational needs for England and Scotland produced by the new Labour Government have slightly different inflections. Both emphasise the needs of the individual child and partnership with parents, but the English document promotes placement in mainstream as the preferred option on moral as well as education grounds, whilst the Scottish document places more emphasis on diversity of provision.

The principles of inclusion and choice: the perspective of the disability movement

To understand this shift in English policy on special educational needs, we need to take into account the growing influence of the disability movement which has argued powerfully for the abolition of separate provision for children with special educational needs since this represents a major barrier to the attainment of equality by disabled children (Barnes 1991, Mason 1993). Informed by the thinking of the disability movement, the Centre for Studies on Integration in Education (CSIE) has promoted integrated provision by publishing statistics charting patterns in the placement of children with special educational needs and producing accounts of inclusive education in action. In a CSIE booklet published in 1990, Shaw (1990) described a visit to the Hamilton and Waterloo School Boards in Canada, where the goal is 'to meet the needs of all children in ordinary, age-appropriate classes in neighbourhood schools'. Special schools in Hamilton and Waterloo have been closed and special classes attached to mainstream schools reduced in number. Even the existence of special classes is being challenged under provincial Human Rights Codes and the Canadian Charter of Rights and Freedoms on the grounds that:

> 'The research since 1980 is very clear. Both academically and socially kids do better in integrated settings than in segregated settings – stuff good teachers have known all their lives.' (Phil Difrancesco, Co-ordinator of special education programmes at Hamilton)

It is also seen as a 'pressing human rights issue':

> 'Change the label. Say black instead of disabled and see if anybody would tolerate those kinds of statements. It's straightforward prejudice.' (Jim Hansen, Director of Education at Waterloo Board)

Shaw questioned why the policy of 'zero exclusion' goes far beyond the tentative approaches to integration which have been attempted to date in the UK and suggests the following explanation:

> the main difference is that Hamilton and Waterloo made a policy commitment to end segregation and planned and organised changes to their education services so they could work towards fulfilling their goal. (Shaw 1990, p. 19)

This approach is in sharp contrast with that adopted by some Scottish authorities, where the policy of inclusion has led to an expansion, not reduction, of special bases attached to mainstream schools. Some organisations have suggested that there is currently too much emphasis on choice and diversity and there is a need for a more directive national strategy. For example, the Council for Disabled Children (established under the aegis of the National Children's Bureau), in its draft policy statement on integration (July 1994) proposed that 'LEAs must be able to exercise a strategic overview of the emergence of increased integration opportunities within their localities' (p. 4).

An interesting feature of the accounts of CSIE and the Council for Disabled Children is the way in which they deal with the principle of choice. Implicit in national and regional policy documents in Scotland is that the right of individual parents to choose appropriate forms of education for their children should be given priority over the planning of integrated provision and the focusing of resources to this end. Implicit in the statements of members of the disability movement is that the principle of integration/inclusion has precedence over the claims of individual parents to make proxy choices on their children's behalf. It is assumed that all parents want integrated provision for their children and those who opt for special schools do so only because resources in mainstream are inadequate. However, a closer look at the arguments of the disability movement suggests that not everybody is in accordance with this view. Corker (1998), for example, describes the historical tensions between deaf culture and the disability movement, as deaf people struggle to achieve cultural autonomy based on the use of sign language, often suppressed in mainstream schools or regarded as inferior to the oralist tradition. Separate academic environments for deaf children are seen as essential for them to master sign language. Recognising the power of these claims, the disability movement generally concedes that this group represents an exception to the rule of integrated provision for all. There is less sympathy, and sometimes outright hostility, however, to parents and voluntary organisations who demand specialised educational provision as the best form of rehabilitation (see, for instance, Oliver's (1989) criticisms of conductive education). The difficulty for the disability movement is that it is clearly problematic to allow the claims of some groups for specialist, segregated provision but disregard the demands of other groups. Furthermore, it is evident that advocates of both inclusion and choice have focused on the wishes of adults, rather than children. Accessing the views and desires of disabled children, although generally regarded as 'a good thing', has not been pursued very actively in education.

To summarise thus far, the principles of integration and choice are treated very differently in official policy documents and the writing of the disability movement. Within official discourse, integration is generally recognised as a valid goal, but the wishes of parents are seen as taking priority over the desire to run the school system along integrated lines. The disability movement has a different set of priorities based on the pursuit of rights for disabled people. The choices of radical parents (that is, those wishing the system to become more clearly inclusive) are seen as legitimate, but parents supporting a separate special system of education, apart from parents of deaf children, would be seen as profoundly misguided and therefore ignored. For the disability movement, the principle of inclusion is generally prioritised over that of choice.

Consequences of the tension between integration/inclusion and choice

Official statistics and patterns of placement

Given the commitment of most education authorities in Scotland to educate children with special educational needs in the least restrictive environment or in integrated settings, one would have expected to see a gradual rise in the rate of integration. In the decade between 1983 and 1993, there was an increase in the number of pupils with Records of Needs, currently about 2 per cent of the school population compared with 3 per cent of pupils with Statements of Need in England. Between 1995 and 1996, there was a 3 per cent increase in the number of children with Records of Needs. In addition, between 1983 and 1993 there was a big increase (from 6% to 42%) in the proportion of pupils with Records of Needs educated in mainstream settings. Since regional reorganisation in 1996, the proportion in mainstream schools has continued to increase and now represents 57 per cent of the total number of pupils with a Record of Needs. Disregarding the small island authorities of Orkney, Shetland and Western Isles, considerable variation is apparent between authorities with a high proportion of recorded pupils in mainstream (for example, that of Dumfries and Galloway) and those with a relatively low proportion (Fife, and Glasgow). Care needs to be taken in interpreting these figures, since authorities which only record those with the most severe difficulties are likely to have a higher proportion of such pupils in special schools. Although there has been an increase in the number of pupils with Records of Needs, there is general consistency within authorities with regard to the proportion of children they place in mainstream. There are no authorities which have shifted from low use of mainstream to high use of mainstream placements for recorded children. Thus rural authorities like Dumfries and Galloway, which placed a relatively high percentage of pupils in mainstream school in 1983, continued to do so. Although national figures suggest an increased use of mainstream, it is not clear whether children who might once have been placed in special are now being placed in mainstream, or whether the increased use of mainstream placements reflects the fact that children with less severe difficulties, who previously would have been supported in mainstream without a Record of Needs, are now being recorded.

In order to answer this question, we need to look at the proportion of the age group being placed in special schools. Although numbers of children in special school have fluctuated, the proportion of the school age population in special school has remained remarkably consistent at about 1 per cent of the population. Here as well, however, interpretation of the data is not entirely straightforward because the Scottish Office category of special placement includes special classes, bases and units. Between 1983 and 1993, the number of special schools in Scotland decreased from 213 to 159 and the number of special units increased from 108 to 168. In some authorities, Grampian for example, the number of special departments increased from 6 to 18 over this period. In Aberdeen City, a successor authority to Grampian Region, the shift towards special bases has continued. In 1996, at the time of local authority reorganisation, there were six bases in the city. Between 1996 and 1999, 14 new bases were opened bringing the total to 22. Inclusion is a central principle informing Aberdeen City's SEN policy, interpreted in the following way:

The principle of inclusion implies an initial assumption that normally each child will be educated in the local community. (Aberdeen City Council 1996, p. 8)

However, as Table 7.1 shows, Aberdeen City appears to be low in its use of mainstream and high in its use of special placements. In the absence of data on the extent to which children in special bases are integrated into the

Table 7.1 Levels of recording and patterns of placement in children with special educational needs in Scotland

Scotland

High recording authorities 1997 (nationally 1.9%)			
Glasgow City	2.9	Aberdeen City	2.5
Dundee City	2.7	Inverclyde	2.5
Renfrewshire	2.7		

Low recording authorities 1997 (nationally 1.9%)			
Orkney Islands	0.8	East Lothian	0.9
West Dunbartonshire	0.8	West Lothian	0.9
East Dunbartonshire	0.9		

High mainstreaming authorities 1997 (nationally 55%)			
East Renfrewshire	61	South Ayrshire	57
Orkney Islands	58	Inverclyde	55
North Ayrshire	57	Eilean Siar	54

Low mainstreaming authorities 1997 (nationally 55%)			
Fife	10	Glasgow City	21
West Lothian	16	Aberdeenshire	25
Aberdeen City	20	Falkirk	29

High use of special schools 1997 (nationally 1%)			
Glasgow City	2.1	South Lanarkshire	1.3
City of Edinburgh	1.6	Clackmannanshire	1.2
Aberdeen City	1.5	Midlothian	1.2

Low use of special schools 1997 (nationally 1%)			
Eilean Siar	0	Shetland Islands	0.1
Dumfries & Galloway	0.1	Moray	0.2
Scottish Borders	0.1	Perth & Kinross	0.2

Source: Scottish Office Education and Industry Department

mainstream, there appears to be a degree of ambiguity in relation to the rhetoric of the policy and its representation through official statistics. A study of mainstream and special school provision (Allan, Brown and Riddell 1995) indicates a wide variety of practice in relation to the amount of integration taking place in special units. It is clearly the case that placement in a special unit does not in itself guarantee a greater degree of integration than education in a special school.

Overall, then, although the figures point to a significant increase in the number of children with Records of Needs in mainstream classes, there is little evidence that there has been a significant decrease in the overall proportion of children placed in the special sector.

Tensions between choice and integration/inclusion: how parents negotiate the system

As we noted above, whilst the disability movement promotes integration as the overarching principle in determining provision, national government policy maintains that parental preferences should be regarded as sovereign. Within many education authority policies, commitment is maintained both to honouring these preferences and therefore maintaining a range of provision, but at the same time to pursuing a policy of integration. Inevitably tensions arise between these different imperatives and in the previous section we considered the lack of movement towards integration suggested by national statistics. In this section we explore the way in which a group of parents experienced the tension between integration/inclusion and choice. If individual parental choices are to be the ultimate arbiters of provision, then it is important to understand on what basis these are made and what effect they are likely to have on the shape of provision.

The case studies referred to here were conducted as part of a study of the effectiveness of mainstream and special school provision for children with special educational needs (Allan, Brown and Riddell 1995). After analysing national statistics on patterns of placement and linking these with regional policy statements, two authorities were selected with distinctively different approaches to provision. Authority E was mainly rural with a few small towns and one major city. Its policy was to develop special units attached to mainstream and there had been considerable growth in their number during the period 1983–93. However, during this period the number of special schools had only fallen by two. Authority Q was mainly urban in character, with a conurbation of industrial towns close to a large city. During the late 1960s and early 1970s, there had been considerable investment in special schools and relatively few special units were in existence. Within each authority, pairs of pupils of similar ages and with broadly similar difficulties were selected, one of whom was placed in mainstream and one of whom was placed in special. A period of time was spent observing each pupil in class and discussing his or her educational experiences with parents, teachers and other professionals. This case study approach clearly did not allow broad generalisations to be made about the comparative educational experiences and attainments of children in mainstream and special schools, partly because of the considerable differences among the pupils in our loosely grouped pairs. The approach did, however, permit the identification of the critical variables having a bearing on placement decisions and subsequent experiences. In the following paragraphs we identify some of the central parameters within which choice of integrated or segregated provision occurs.

There appeared to be marked variation among parents between those who were able to articulate their choice of school with professionals and those who were not able to do this. Generally, parents who were able to persuade professionals of the validity of their claims were middle class. The salience of social class was illustrated in relation to two children with Down's syndrome, Brian who was placed in mainstream for his primary education, and Tony who was placed in special. Even though Brian's pre-school psychological assessment was rather negative, his professional mother and father argued strongly that their son should spend the early years of his education in the local village primary. His mother explained:

> 'Middleton is a relatively small place and my husband and I didn't see why Brian should be bussed out of the area until he's about 16 and then arrive back here and nobody knows him. Whereas now we go down to the town and it's 'Hi Brian, hi Brian'. He goes to Sunday school and boys' brigade.'

The Record of Needs provided testimony of professional approval of the parents, who were described as 'intelligent caring people who have provided a richly stimulating home environment for him. They are anxious to pursue a positive approach which has obviously contributed greatly to Brian's development.' The head teacher was in no doubt as to why Brian's parents had been successful in countering the psychologist's argument that the boy would be better off in special:

> 'I think really it is only because they are very well educated, articulate people that they are able to fight their case. I'm sure had they been people who had easily been put down or pushed aside things would have gone in the other direction. I would say they knew their rights and fought their case and that is why Brian is still here.'

Both the headteacher and the class teacher were still doubtful about the success of the placement, feeling that Brian would have got 'something special' (although they were not sure what that might have been) in a special school. Although Brian's parents had won the fight for an integrated placement in primary school, they had, somewhat reluctantly, agreed to a placement in a special unit attached to a mainstream secondary for Brian's secondary education:

> 'It would be great if there was a unit in Middleton Academy, then he could go on with the children he knows, but unfortunately not, so it's out of the question. I feel a bit concerned that he'll see a lot of handicapped children ... Johnson is really the best of a bad bunch.'

By way of contrast, Tony, from a working class background, started his educational career in a school for children with moderate learning difficulties and was subsequently transferred to a school for pupils with severe learning difficulties. At the time of the interview, Tony was 15, and, looking back, his mother wished that she had insisted on an integrated placement:

> 'I never ever tried to get Tony into a normal school. Sometimes I wish I had but then I felt that kids were cruel and I was frightened. I didn't know how Tony was going to turn out. Looking at him now, I wish I had tried to get him into a normal school.'

Having three sons close together, she had always treated Tony the same as her other boys. In the eyes of the psychologist, this represented both a potential problem because it indicated a failure to recognise Tony's problems. The psychologist's assessment in the Record of Needs recognised the affectionate and caring nature of Tony's home, but continued:

> Difficulties have arisen because of Tony's lack of progress in formal schoolwork. Mrs M has been very frustrated by this and is struggling to come to terms with the cognitive limitations of Tony's handicap and her need to change her approach to him ... Until Mrs M adjusts to the limitations of Tony's cognitive ability she may well be disappointed with his progress at Budmouth [school for children with severe learning difficulties].

Mrs M was still indignant that her refusal to treat Tony as 'an ill person' had been seen as abnormal by the psychologist, but despite her indignation she had seen no alternative but to acquiesce with professional judgements.

Among our case studies it was evident that choice represented a strategy strongly dependent on social class. However, middle class parents did not always wish for their child to be educated in mainstream. In Authority E, another of our case studies was of Catherine, a girl with Down's Syndrome about to enter secondary. Her mother was adamant that she did not wish a placement in a special base because her daughter might be in danger from the other children and would not get enough specialist input. Although the authority was trying to close the special school which Catherine's mother wished her to attend, the placing request was acceded to.

Geography and the established pattern of local authority provision were also factors influencing Tony and Brian's placements. Living in an urban area with many special schools, a mainstream placement for Tony might have been seen as distorting the authority's budget because of the need to resource two distinctive types of provision. For Brian, living in a rural area, placement in a mainstream primary with additional support might have been seen as a cheaper option than a special school placement which would have involved the cost of transport. Furthermore, although children with certain 'types' of SEN were liable to be placed in either mainstream or special settings, those with profound or multiple difficulties were almost invariably placed in special settings irrespective of the parents' social class, the authority's geography, policy and established pattern of provision.

Conclusion

Tensions between the principles of integration/inclusion and choice have characterised special educational needs policy in the UK for two decades. Comparing special educational needs policy documents of the 1970s and early 1990s, we find a shift away from the idea of partnership with parents towards the notion of parents as consumers, albeit less powerful than parents of non-disabled children. Integration, identified by Warnock as the favoured option, occupies a less prominent position in Conservative special educational needs policy, despite strong lobbying by the disability movement. New Labour policy documents in England herald a decisive shift towards integration/inclusion, whilst in Scotland, policy statements highlight the needs of the individual child and partnership with parents. Attempting to run a system based on the principles of integration and choice appears to have produced a state of policy stasis. Despite the presence of more children with Records of Needs in mainstream, there is no evidence of a reduction in the proportion of the age group in the special sector. To make matters more complicated, authorities which have shifted their provision from special schools to special units or bases claim that this counts as inclusion, although the amount of time that children in special bases spend with their mainstream peers varies enormously.

Case study data provide insight into how parents of children with special educational needs experienced the twin principles of integration and choice. It was evident that a pure market did not exist within which parents were free to choose between integrated and segregated options. Rather, choice was structured by regional policy, geography, social class and nature of the child's impairment. Ball (1993) maintained that the implementation of market reforms in education is essentially 'a class strategy which has as one of its major effects the reproduction of relative social class (and ethnic) advantages and disadvantages' (p. 4). In the sphere of special educational needs, it is evident that opportunities are structured not only by social class but by a much wider range of factors including the nature of the child's impairment.

Tensions between integration and choice within special educational needs policy reveal an underlying tension between individualism and collectivism. The previous Conservative government almost always came down on the side of individualism, although, as Jonathan (1993) noted:

> A market in education creates a competitive framework in which parents as consumers can seek relative advantage for their children. But it also creates a situation in which each child becomes vulnerable to the unspecifiable effects of the aggregate choices of other children's proxies. (p. 21)

In special educational needs, this is particularly apparent. If parents reject special schools, these swiftly become too expensive to run. By the same token, investment in the infrastructure of mainstream depends on enough parents choosing this option. In many parts of Scotland, running parallel systems of special educational provision, one based in special and one in mainstream, may be necessary to give parents and children a choice of provision, but is likely to be seen as incompatible with the effective and efficient use of resources. If a decision is made to shift more resources into mainstream provision, then some parents are likely to feel short-changed and may start to seek legal redress. Unlike England, where Special Educational Needs Tribunals exist, Scottish parents have limited avenues for appeal and have been rather reluctant to make use of them. However, a tilting of national and local policy towards inclusion in mainstream rather than separate special provision might lead to more conflict within the special educational needs arena. As the new Scottish Parliament gets underway, special educational needs will undoubtedly be an area of major policy importance, highlighting, as it does, uneasy tensions between parental choice, a major policy motif of the previous government, and inclusion, a major theme of the present government.

Chapter 8

Special education in today's Sweden – a struggle between the Swedish model and the market

Bengt Persson

Introduction

Special education is an integral part of the comprehensive school system in Sweden. From 1962 when Sweden established its first National Curriculum, along with its comprehensive school for all, the amount of special education steadily increased until the middle of the 1970s. To this end the concept of integration has remained generally unchallenged among politicians as well as the public at large. As a consequence of this the numbers of special schools and special classes have been drastically reduced and most special education now takes place within the comprehensive schools.

This chapter will briefly engage with the following issues:

- A brief historical survey of the development of Swedish special education from a remedial tool of education into a preventive one.
- Today's policy and practice concerning the concepts of integration and segregation in relation to current political trends in Sweden and the present change to the educational system.
- Some results from a recently finished research project (Special Education in the Comprehensive School – A study of its prerequisites, practice and direction of action) at Göteborg University.
- The importance of comparative work within the field of education.
- A discussion and analysis of special education in Sweden in relationship to future needs and public resources.

Society and deviance from a philosophical view

Integration, normalisation and inclusion are constructs very much related to modern Western society and often linked with some kind of activity either from an institution or from the individual in order to create some sense of community. As this is seldom emotive, even the most deserving attempts to 'integrate' disabled people into some kind of institutional setting can be unsuccesful. However, today's situation has not always been the case. One of those who investigated the issues of divergence from what could be called 'normal' was the French philosopher Michel Foucault. In his doctor's dissertation *Madness and Civilization* (1967) Foucault reviews the state of tension between reason and insanity and problematises the way in which deviance is reified in definitions, professions and institutions.

Foucault's point of departure is that deviants are usually thought of as being relatively rare and therefore the other (i.e. normal) people, by virtue of being in the majority, have the right to make decisions concerning the lives of the deviants. Through regarding deviance as something that exists within some other individuals, we exclude insanity from our own lives even though every person has some part of himself which could be defined as 'mad'.

Foucault then gives an historical presentation of madness in different cultures from around 1450 to the present time, ending with 'the Birth of the Clinic'. Here, in the 'clinic', the deviant is placed on the same footing as the sick and is, therefore, to be treated by doctors or other experts. This implies that they have to be segregated from society and thus not accessible for the interventions of normal people. To summarise Foucault's theories, the deviant plays the role of the segregated, excluded and scoffed at. This is, however, not a meaningless role. On the contrary the presence of the deviant is important in the social system – a part of the frame of reference that society and social life needs. He represents that which has to be treated differently in order for the normal to consolidate their roles as normal. In contrast to the sick and the relationship between the sick patient and doctor – that is, between two individuals, this conception of the deviant creates a new relationship – one between society and human beings. Foucault's first analyses from the 1950s showed that madness cannot be understood from within itself but from the world around and the epistemological milieu which defines it.

Now, what has Foucault and his definitions of madness and deviance got to do with education in the 1990s? The answer seems to be not too remote. Most educational systems have traditionally developed settings where teachers were to teach only the educable. Those who appeared to have difficulties in coping with the demands of school were often treated separately, which in turn contributed to the perception of them as deviants. Even if the policies of inclusion and integration are prestige words of today, strong reactionary forces counteract such policies. One significant example of this is the following statement made by the former Swedish Minister of Schools, Beatrice Ask, shortly after the change of government in 1991:

> We also have to talk openly about problems in today's schools. There are so many pregnant fields that nobody dares to deal with properly. One of those fields is pupils with difficulties, e.g. I myself think that integration

has gone too far, in a way that is good for no one. But I know that this is a delicate subject to talk about. (*Lärarnas Tidning*, 1991, p. 6)

Why special education?

Special education in the Swedish school can best be understood in relationship to the democratic process in Swedish society, making it a political/ideological question. According to the School Act of 1842, poor children as well as those who lacked the necessary talent were only allowed access to minimum courses at school. These courses became highly criticised especially because of their disadvantages for the lower social classes. This critique peters out in 1897 when it was decreed that only mentally retarded pupils would be subjected to minimum courses (Söder 1984, p. 12). Around the turn of the century there were many lively debates as to whether the presence of 'weak and depraved' children was detrimental to the reputation of the public school. Many teachers' view was that 'intellectually deficient children' appeared to impede school lessons and were therefore 'a detriment to the normal children' (Stukát and Bladini 1986, p. 3).

With reference to Rosenqvist (1993) three different periods can be discerned in the history of special education in Sweden: (a) the stage of non-differentiation; (b) the stage of differentiation; (c) the stage of integration. I will use Rosenqvist's classification but extend it with a fourth stage due to the rapid change in Swedish society during the 1990s.

(a) The non-differentiation stage lasted until the turn of the century, or, to be more realistic, until around 1950 for most mentally retarded children. Before then many children, notwithstanding the fact that they were allowed to attend school, had to repeat grades or leave school. There were however many disabled children who were kept hidden by their families and thus never gained access to school.

(b) The second period overlaps the first one. In the middle of the 19th century schools for deaf, blind and mentally retarded children were started mainly as charitable institutions and in the case of Miss Emanuella Carlbeck's 'Idiot School' in Göteborg, with governmental financial support.

After 1905 the number of special classes and remedial classes grew rapidly (Table 8.1). Pupils were selected to special education in special classes with the help of doctors' and teachers' judgements as well as by using IQ tests. The 1957 school committee (SOU 1961, p. 30) proposed a differential system of special education. The philosophy at this period was the belief that the pupil was the cause of their school problems and therefore should be taught in a way that matched up with the specific difficulties shown. In the first Swedish National Curriculum (Lgr 62), the contents and organisation of special education were carefully specified and the

Table 8.1 The growth of special education (special classes) in Sweden 1907–1935 (Stukát and Bladini 1986, p. 4)

	Number of school districts with special classes	Number of special classes	Number of pupils
1907	15	39	266
1923	51	179	2,815
1928	60	224	3,190
1935	70	264	3,794

accompanying proposal was for a system of coordinated special education as an alternative to remedial and special classes.

(c) The integration phase was initiated in the revised National Curriculum 1969 (Lgr 69) and proposed that special education should be coordinated with regular instruction within the classroom. The Swedish National Board of Education (SÖ) also fixed a maximum limit for special education in schools of 0.3 hours per week per pupil meaning that on average each special teacher supported four classes. This should be seen as a manifestation of the idea of integration as well as a strong reaction against the earlier segregated provision of special education.

The 1969 curriculum recommended an increased integration of pupils with various forms of disabilities into regular classes. It was also noted that the individual school's environment, organisation and instructional methods were possible causes of the pupil's difficulties in fulfilling the demands of the school.

The National Curriculum of 1980 (Lgr 80) attempted to reduce the difference between special education and regular education. The most important goal in the 1980 plan was to *prevent the child from having difficulties in school*. In addition, the Lgr 80 underscores the importance of the individual child who receives help in a special education group to return to his or her regular group. The rationale for this is the belief that learning in a heterogeneous group is more effective than in a homogeneous one.

Since 1962 the amount of special education has grown steadily in the Swedish compulsory school. Critics claimed that this was a signal that a single compulsory school cannot cope with teaching all children. Instead, they argued, when this is attempted, a number of children are filtered out and educated in small groups with special methods parallel to the regular education in the classroom. The number of special teachers steadily increased and there appeared to be an unspoken agreement between the class teachers and the special teachers which allowed special education to increase resources. Kivirauma and Kivinen (1988) described this phenomenon in the following way:

Not a single professional group within the field of education has considered it necessary to oppose the expansionism of special education. Why should they? Special education lightens the work load of teachers in ordinary classes by offering more or less permanent solutions (such as transfer to special education classes or therapy in a clinic) to the problem of difficult students. (p. 160)

A new sphere of action for special education

In 1986 the Social Democratic government presented a report concerning special education in the comprehensive school system. The investigators suggested a number of measures to improve the situation:

- A new extended special education teacher's university programme[1].
- A change in the duties of the teacher of special education.
- A decrease in teaching time so that the special educational teacher could devote more time to consultant tasks.
- An extended field of responsibility for the special education teacher, including the initiating and managing of local school development work.

The government passed this legislation in 1989 and in the autumn of 1990 the new teacher's education programme for special educators began at four universities in Sweden. A very noticeable change in the professional tasks were the new non-teaching duties. The new programme includes instruction in giving guidance to other teachers who experience problems in their role as teacher.

This new legislation caused much agitation and frustration among the country's special teachers. Many felt their positions were threatened and that the changes implied that the work they had been carrying out for many years was now seen as worthless. Their immediate reactions were sometimes very strong and suspicion concerning the consequenses of implementing the legislation continues to be noticeable. Ahl, Nyberg and Persson (1994), who investigated the work situation among 60 special educators who graduated in 1992 wrote:

Many of the interviewees claim that special teachers (holding the old type of diploma) experience their position as being threatened by the special educator. However, a situation characterised by competition need not arise between these two professional categories. On the contrary it should be possible to take advantage of the different educational skills and knowledge that the two groups have gained in different ways. (p. 25)

A new national curriculum including all children

In July 1995 a new national curriculum was introduced in Sweden. In contrast with the former plan, this new plan takes a different standpoint in relation to teachers, head teachers and special educators. Instead of prescribing methods for the professionals in schools, attainment goals are set up at the national level for pupils to reach by the end of the fifth and ninth year at school. The Ministry of Education and Science then presupposes that teachers will use appropriate methods in order to reach the goals within this system. Head teachers will be answerable to parliament for achievement of the goals – a responsibility which is expressed in the following way concerning children with special needs:

> The head teacher has overall responsibility for the activity as a whole being oriented to the attainment of the nationally determined goals. The head teacher has, as a result, within the framework set out, special responsibility for
> * education and pupil social welfare being organised such that pupils needing special assistance and help receive this. (Lpo 94, p. 17)

Swedish teachers have by tradition been expected to place reliance on regulations and directives from the National Board of Education. However, within the framework of the new national curriculum they will find themselves having greater autonomy in their work, coupled with new responsibilities relating to pupil achievement.

Another modulation is the division of responsibility for the schools which means a clearer demarcation between national and local levels and between those whose task is to decide on the goals of the activity – local politicians, and those whose task is to work for its implementation, for example head teachers in the schools. The new goal and results–orientation also means that schools should no longer be steered principally by rules and regulations set nationally, but rather by nationally determined goals. Teachers, head teachers and pupils will be responsible for transforming these into educational goals and in this way draw up their own local work plan as a kind of participatory goal steering.

The nationally determined goals have two principally different objectives. 'Perspective Goals' are goals to be strived for and worked towards. They need not necessarily be attained in their entirety, but they provide a focus for instruction. In contrast 'Attainment Goals' specify the knowledge that all pupils should be guaranteed in the compulsory school. The evaluation of these goals after the fifth year at school is important for children with special educational needs as it will serve as a basis for possible reallocation of resources. However, allocation of resources according to the new state grant system has already caused difficulties. In some municipalities budgets for special education have been cut by as much as 50 per cent (Persson 1994, p. 9).

Inclusive education is the foundation upon which the Swedish compulsory school is built. Inclusion therefore means that each pupil has the same right to obtain knowledge and skills at school as every other pupil. However society's demands that schools evaluate pupils' knowledge and skills seem to cause conflicts in the school situation. On the one hand pupils should be trained to cooperate and build their own knowledge in relation to their prerequisites while on the other hand this knowledge that they acquire is to be measured. It goes without saying that pupils who experience difficulties at school notwithstanding hard work, will get the least attractive marks.

Market oriented segregation

The shift of paradigm in the Swedish educational system leads to an extension of Rosenqvist's three stages by a fourth stage, namely the market oriented segregation phase. By this concept I mean the consequence of the dismantling of the Swedish Model[2] and the increasing influence of market ideologies on the public sector. Within this model the Swedish education system managed to maintain a balance between public and private interests where education for the good of the public was emphasised. During the present period, which can be characterised by individualisation, market orientation and internationalisation, education includes the right of parents to decide upon the socialisation values of their children. This change can also be labelled as a direction from *pluralism within the public education system* towards *organised pluralism based on public and private schools*. From the pupil's point of view this means that once the choice is made (by the parents) the pupils will have to accept the consequences. Of course this has a great impact for children whose parents for one reason or another are at a disadvantage in society and therefore not able to choose at all. The long term result of this will no doubt be organised segregation.

During the last few years there have been dramatic budget cut-backs in Swedish schools[3]. The pupil–teacher ratio is increasing and in most municipalities special education receives fewer resources. One obvious tendency is that when the size of classes increases so does segregation; the paradox being that one would suppose that budget cut-backs imply fewer, not more, special settings. However because class teachers have difficulties in handling the individual needs of many pupils on different educational and developmental levels, the solution then is to 'stream' the pupils, meaning that more homogeneous groups are created. Because this is contrary to the proposition in the curriculum, the settings are referred to as temporary. However once you have started streaming it is very demanding to return to a mainstream system.

Nevertheless in all fairness it should be noted that the conservative four part coalition government was aware of the risk of decreasing budgets in the municipalities with respect to children with special educational needs:

> Almost half of all municipalities declare that the number of pupils with special needs has increased. However the priorities for helping this group of pupils have changed owing to decreasing financial resources' demand of economic solutions. The National Agency for Education notes a tendency to allocate resources for special educational needs to fewer and more resource-demanding pupils.

> From this account the government draws the conclusion that there might be a risk that pupils with less evident difficulties or disabilities will not get sufficient support and that this will need further clarification. The government intends to monitor this issue carefully during the next three year period.
> (Skr. 1993/94:183)

An additional problem is segregation at different levels of society. Large cities like Stockholm, Göteborg and Malmö have their 'slum areas' in the suburbs. The class differences are now not only economic but also cultural, ethnic and intellectual. There seems to be a critical point when schools have about 50 per cent of non-Swedish nationals which contributes to a tendency for Swedish people to move to other areas. The empty flats will thereafter be filled with new people, mostly immigrants, refugees or Swedes from the lower social classes. Thus segregation becomes a fact.

Forced integration

Integration is often associated with desirable, positive solutions in schools. The positive factors are twofold: the disabled child gets access and the opportunity to share common societal facilities and be involved in the same environment as the others; all children get a wider frame of reference which will enrich their own lives.

However one has to be very vigilant in times of budget cut-backs. If school head teachers find it difficult to arrange classes in the traditional manner within the budget available, it will of course be tempting to reduce the amount of special education taking place in clinics, resource rooms as well as in the classrooms. The pupils in question may be required then to return to their classes without any support from special education teachers in the name of *integration*. It is then highly probable that the difficulties in the classroom will increase and the so called 'integrated pupils' may be blamed for a deteriorated situation.

It will be interesting to note how the Swedish school system will cope with these new demands. It seems likely that the system works well when society is quite well-off. But what happens to the system in times of high budget cuts? The following paragraph describes what happened in Finland where the economic cut-backs have been even greater than in Sweden. Happonen *et al.* (1994) write:

> Integration as a slogan can, however, get a foothold. It is possible that in the name of integration one transfers pupils who need special education to normal classes, without giving the necessary support and habilitation and without in-service training for the class teacher. It also happens that special education is being brutally abolished for those pupils who get special education occasionally, whilst the numbers of pupils in the classes increase. The result then is that the class teacher without any in-service training at all has to face new problems. (p. 37)

Another aspect not to be neglected is the effects of deregulation and decentralisation in Swedish schools. From having been a top-down centralised system the Swedish educational system has now turned into a bottom-up decentralised system. As mentioned previously, parents are now free to choose even among the public schools for their children. However 'free choice' is not a realistic alternative for children experiencing learning difficulties if the facilities in a school are not adapted to meet the child's needs. It seems reasonable to suppose that schools within a given school district may then cooperate to equip *one* school in the district for enrolling disabled[4] pupils. One does not have to think too far ahead to see that this could become a giant step towards further segregation.

The educational system will now have to show if it can stand the strain. For example, will head teachers feel confident that they can realistically set up long term economic goals in order to develop new strategies for dealing with changing special educational needs? Will teachers get adequate and qualified in-service training so as to acquire new teaching strategies adapted to their changing role as a teacher?

However one must remember that in international comparisons Swedish schools have traditionally been accustomed to substantial economic support. In 1990 the public expenditure on education as a percentage of GNP was 7.7 per cent (World Education Report 1993, p. 151). Among the European countries only Norway showed a higher figure. An optimistic view of the future then would lead us to see the years of frustrating system change succeeded by a stabilised but human system based on reduced and, hopefully, more realistic costs.

Transformation of policies

A common way of describing educational activities at the local level in relation to national goals and intentions, is to use an hierarchical model. Robitaille and Garden (1989) use the concepts *intended, implemented* and *achieved* curriculum while Goodlad (1979) uses similar concepts to describe this hierarchy, namely *ideological, formal, understood, implemented* and *experienced* curriculum.

The model illustrated in Figure 8.1 rests on the idea of the hierarchical order to ideally transform nationally determined goals into lower levels of the educational system. Furthermore it is presumed that within the context of the Swedish decentralised educational system, policy decisions in harmony with the national goals are made at all levels of the system. Even if the municipalities are to some degree autonomous, the ideal and overall aims of the hierarchical model is that goals set nationally are to become transformed into local practice.

However, for such transformations to occur it is presupposed that no competing policies appear in schools and classrooms. These ideal conditions are illustrated in Figure 8.2. The problem seems to be that the power of the local policies might to a considerable degree counteract the national policies which in turn entails schools becoming very different from each other.

In practice this might mean that arbitrariness or pressure from influential groups in the schools strongly influence the aims and content of the local special educational activities. Thus what in one school might be regarded as 'normal behaviour' might in another school be regarded as highly deviant. Such conflicts between different kinds of policies might threaten and even undo the transformation model and contribute to random definitions of the target groups for special education.

During the late 1990s Sweden is experiencing increasing inequality between different groups of people in society. Such inequalities become reflected in schools and manifested in varying academic standards. Persson (1998) shows that more than 16 per cent of the differences in mathematics

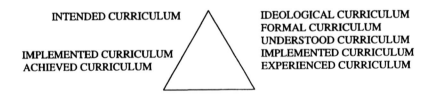

INTENDED CURRICULUM   IDEOLOGICAL CURRICULUM
FORMAL CURRICULUM
UNDERSTOOD CURRICULUM
IMPLEMENTED CURRICULUM   IMPLEMENTED CURRICULUM
ACHIEVED CURRICULUM   EXPERIENCED CURRICULUM

Figure 8.1 Hierarchical model illustrating the transformation of nationally set goals into the achievement of knowledge and skills amoung pupils

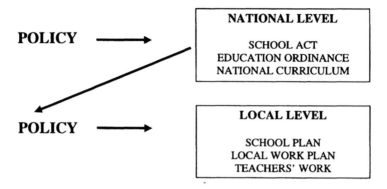

Figure 8.2 The relationship between instruments of control on national and local levels within the educational system

achievement among 12-year-old pupils, is explained by factors at the group level (i.e. differences between schools). Previous research reports that values higher than ten per cent are large in this context. When distribution of special educational resources were analysed in the same way it was found that less than five per cent of the variance was explained at the school level. In order to meet the needs of students in less favoured schools, this resource allocation should be more skewed. Local policies, however, often counteract such legitimate emphasis upon special needs support. Instead resources often become used to reduce the student–teacher ratio in classrooms thereby contributing to facilitating working conditions among teachers, which of course is desirable but not necessarily leading to an improved situation for pupils in need of support.

Special education and its consequences – a research project at Göteborg University

In this section some findings from a research project entitled *Special Education in the Comprehensive School – A study of its prerequisites, practice and direction of action* (Persson 1995) are presented. The aim of this study is to analyse the ways in which different groups of professionals in the Swedish comprehensive school system conceive and describe the special educational activities taking place in their schools. Twenty-seven special educators, 35 classroom teachers and 18 principals were interviewed and local curricula as well as developmental work plans for special education in the investigated schools were collected. The project was initiated in 1992 and the National Agency for Schools awarded a grant the same year. The statements by the interviewees were analysed with respect to differences and similarities before being arranged in categories (representing different qualitative aspects) and groups (representing sets of related categories). In addition, the interviews with the special educators were analysed to determine the focus of their work.

The results indicate that special education activities are highly dependent upon the policies of the local school. When there existed harmonising policies supported by the principals, the special educators were encouraged to widen their focus of work to include not only the pupil, but also the environment encircling the pupil; for example, the class or the entire school and what is more, the ways of planning for and working in regular teaching. However this was extremely rare.

The extent of the special education activities taking place in the schools was highly dependent upon tradition, organisational structure and teaching duties as well as the actual need for help. It also appears that the most common reason for pupils receiving special education is that they exhibit difficulties in reading, writing and mathematics. A major responsibility resting on the special education teachers/educators is to help the class teachers to solve acute situations by separating the pupil from his or her class.

Most of the time spent on special education lessons is devoted to reading and writing with these activities being most common in the upper grades. Systematic evaluation and the drawing up of individual education plans appear to be quite rare.

As mentioned earlier the official goal of the Swedish school policy could be summed up in the concept 'A School for All'. This means that every child should be guaranteed the same right to education irrespective of ancestry, living environment and so forth. However, to work efficiently A School for All seems to need special educators to paper over the cracks. Their work is regulated in official documents ('written policy' to use Fulcher's (1989) words) but our study indicates that stated and enacted policies are far from intentions formulated in curricula and parliamentary resolutions.

One of our findings is that special educators very seldom question the contribution of the environment encircling the pupil to the difficulties shown. Figure 8.3 aims at illustrating the relationships between the focus for the special educational activities and the kind of support given. With few exceptions the special educational activities undertaken can be described by factors in the

	PROTECTING	TAKING ACTION	RESHAPING
SOCIETY			
SCHOOL			
CLASS/GROUP	••••••••••••		
INDIVIDUAL	••••••••••••	••••••••••••	

Figure 8.3 The relationship between factors of significance for the content and focus for special educational activities

marked squares. This means that in its most extreme form, special education aims at protecting the pupil from a hostile reality. Many interviewees claim that pupils, although they definitely do not *need* special education, want to stay in the room where the special educator's classes are held.

In schools where the special educators are supported by the head teacher, it appears to be easier to widen the focus for their work. This, then, implies that it is possible to work preventively, not only with the pupils but also with staff and the educational conditions in the local schools. Actually this was one of the major changes within the field of Swedish special education and was described in the very important Government Bill of 1988 (Prop. 88/89:4, p. 80).

The reader might find it far-fetched to connect this with the market orientation of the Swedish educational system. However in times when every part of schooling has to fight for resources, meaning that special educators have to put forward credible arguments for getting resources in competition with, for example, the mathematics or English teachers, it seems to be difficult for them to identify and point out weaknesses in teaching methods or classroom or school management. It might be much easier to work on adjusting the 'deviant' child to the demands of the teachers or school organisation. The only reasonable way to avoid situations like this seems to be that *head teachers* give their special educators authority to work with special educational tasks within any relevant arena in the local school within a certain cost ceiling. Needless to say, even this task might be a demanding one, but this in turn indicates the importance of well-educated special educators. However, this is a well-known problem even in England. Galloway and Goodwin noted that identifying shortcomings of this kind 'could imply that the teacher, or headteacher has special educational needs, not the child!' (p. 127).

Hand-in-hand with the growing influence from the market goes also a more greatly stressed élite-perspective in the education field. In our research project we found statements that most probably would not have been expressed only a few years ago. Some interviewees claim that it might be unprofitable to use teaching time for children for whom the benefits appear to be very few. One primary school teacher said:

> Is it really meaningful to give special education to hopeless pupils, pupils we feel it meaningless to waste time on? They don't learn anything anyway. It's time to put provocative questions even at school. I think, even if it is horrible to say, that we'll have to cut down resources for them. We'll have to give them up a little ... (Persson 1995, p. 73)

Many interviewees take up controversial issues like these in relation to budget cut-backs in schools. They express the opinion that the aim must be to get value for money which of course implies that it is wasted time to give children with for example learning disabilities additional support or help.

However, this is a question of equal opportunities, an issue that is one of the mainstays underpinning the Swedish educational system. But equal opportunities does not mean that everyone gets the same. On the contrary it means that those who need most should get most. This is declared in the Swedish School Act and must not be ignored by anyone, and especially not by school staff.

Special education and future research

Rosenqvist (1994) has investigated, on behalf of the National Agency for Education, Swedish research projects (within the area of special education and disability) carried out during the last ten years. Rosenqvist questions the narrow aims and directions of the projects investigated and writes:

> Most of these projects have a clear but unidentified point of departure in a kind of labelling of different kinds of deviance. This conception is certainly quite common among people but research ought to devote more energy to calling into question conventions of what is commonly considered as deviance. (p. 41)

Rosenqvist points out an important weakness in today's research and developmental work within the special education field. Deviance is implicitly regarded as an absolute entity and research tends to aim at facilitating living conditions among deviant people *given* their deviance. However deviance is defined by the so called normal (see p. 117) and is highly dependent upon values, policies and ideologies.

The Swedish parental organisation for children with learning difficulties (FUB) has made an inventory of ongoing projects within this field (Riksförbundet FUB 1994). Among the projects described I examined 82 descriptions of projects carried out at universities or research foundations in Sweden. Most projects aim at developing methods (computer software, technical aids), albeit very few, which try to investigate the relationship between the impairment (or handicapping condition) and the environment. Instead future research has to problematise disability in relation to changes in society as a whole.

Comparative work – promises and problems

In this chapter I have tried to describe a universal problem (schools' difficulties in handling deviance) in the Swedish national context. Comparative work is a well-established way of conducting cross-national studies and of identifying, describing and analysing similarities and differences across societies. The benefits of such work is obvious – it makes it possible for us to get deeper understanding of other cultures and national systems. A growing internationalisation and globalisation have involved researchers and politicians in becoming more interested in international comparisons particularly in the area of education as a means of evaluating solutions for dealing with common problems such as special needs support.

Such comparisons, however, are too often superficial, based as they are on statistics collected from national administrative bodies. A recent example of this is the European Commission report *Provision for Pupils with Special Educational Needs* (Meijer 1998). The need for streamlining carries the risk of collecting invalid data as they are related to certain national conditions and contexts and also to an historical development which is frequently overlooked. An example of such complexities is the definition of what kind of provisions special needs education refers to. Hegarty (1991) writes that:

> Estimates of the number of pupils served by special education in different countries vary widely. A Unesco survey found that, in 51 countries supplying information, the proportion of the school-age population enrolled in special education ranged from less than 0.1% to 13%. (p. 89)

Hegarty takes the Scandinavian countries as examples of the problems surrounding definitions and terminology. While the Danish authorities reported 13 per cent of all students as receiving some kind of special education, the corresponding Norwegian figure was 0.7 per cent. The Swedish authorities reported that it was impossible to answer the question because of the unclear boundaries between special and regular education.

Despite such problems, comparative work has significant importance especially if the analyses focus on underlying and sometimes invisible factors. Hantrais (1996) captures the advantages of comparative work when she writes that:

> Cross-national comparativists are forced to attempt to adopt a different cultural perspective, to learn to understand the thought processes of another culture and to see it from the native's viewpoint, while also reconsidering their own country from the perspective of a skilled, external observer. (p. 4)

Conclusion

To sum up I will highlight some issues relating to the responsibilities resting on teacher training and especially the training of special educators. As mentioned earlier, these programmes have undergone a thorough change during the last five to six years in Sweden. However teacher training, like regular education in schools, is burdened by traditions, conflicts, loyalties and coalitions that hamper innovations and confirm yesterday's courses of action. The training of special educators is one of the most important factors for a sound development within the special education field. The crucial point is whether the 'deviant' child will or will not be transferred to special settings or treated by educational specialists. This is what Fulcher (1989, p. 9) calls the *divisive discourse* opposed to the *inclusive discourse*. If we accept that the ordinary classroom is the best place for all children then we also accept that the role of special educators has to change. I assert that the kind of competence required is characterised by being a generalist rather than a specialist. This then means that all teachers should have the ability to understand, analyse and contribute to changes in teaching situations, classroom, school organisation and so forth. Even if this might be a heavy demand and sometimes perhaps fraught with conflict, this seems to be the only way forward if our aim is real inclusion.

Notes

1. On comparison with the English system the Swedish programme is equal to 160 credits.
2. Englund (1993) describes the Swedish Model as an 'era characterised by strong public sector expansion, centralised collective bargaining based on an historic compromise between labour and capital, social engineering and centrally planned standard solutions'.
3. Cost accounts for schools for the period 1990–92 indicates that the core activity, teaching, receives ever decreasing funding while costs for premises are increasing and administrative costs are virtually constant. (Ds 1994:56, p. 136)
4. This might be a problem mainly for pupils who have slight learning or motor disabilities who have reading or writing difficulties, for example.

Chapter 9

An international conversation on inclusive education

Jenny Corbett and Roger Slee

The rules for engagement

This book provides a most welcome opportunity for two friends and workers in the field of Inclusive Education [bell hooks, 1994 refers to this as cultural worker] to meet together to catch up and talk about where the movement is up to. Specifically, it allows us to listen to descriptions of developments in our respective countries as policy continues to grapple with the cultural requirements that underwrite the project of inclusive schooling.

The immediate inclination is to produce a predictable comparative chapter where we describe one country's policy, followed by the other and then write a conclusion that includes exhortations for developments in the future. We have determined that we will attempt to allow our readers to eavesdrop, to come into the room and listen to an unfolding conversation on inclusive education. In these most post-structural of days we will offer some guidance for what we are attempting to do.

Our opening will take the shape of a series of conceptual reflections about inclusion. An 'in vogue' term these days, we need to issue cautions about its generalisation and potential for misuse. We will then reflect upon inclusive education in England and Wales and in Australia by addressing a series of questions:

- How can schools create an inclusive culture in a climate of educational markets and school effectiveness?
- Are the concepts of entitlement and inclusion incompatible?
- What does inclusion actually involve?
- What specific practices help individuals to feel included or excluded?

This will be pursued as a conversation where we allow each other the opportunity to respond to each other's statements about each of those questions. The final part of this chapter attempts to consider these statements about inclusion in nation states as a series of global and local themes.

Inclusive education – what is it?

Inclusive education is not another bureaucratic discourse for surveilling and managing disabled or the so-called 'special educational needs students' into and out of regular schools. We have witnessed the growth of a most dynamic conversation between a whole range of constituencies about their identities and the collision of their differences with present forms of educational delivery. The *International Journal of Inclusive Education* is an example of where people have been encouraged to write about major issues in education, and their experience of schooling, training and higher education from their particular vantage points. People write about the experiences of students and education workers from different ethnicities and language backgrounds, from different sexual identities, as disabled people, about educational and social exclusion in different national and regional contexts and across different educational sectors. Significantly, the writing grapples with both issues of student and professional identities. Inclusion, it would seem, is about cultural synergies for an ever broadening range of human identities.

This quite properly leads into our second observation about inclusive education. Inclusive education is an unabashed announcement, a public and political declaration and celebration of difference. Difference is not a euphemism for defect, for abnormality, for a problem to be worked out through technical and assimilationist education policies (Branson and Miller 1987). Diversity is a social fact. It would appear that the development of education systems has been predicated by the denial of the existence and value of difference. School cultures have been mono-dimensional in their establishment of the strictures of traditional academic male, Anglophile curricular, pedagogy and school organisation. Turning this around is not a project for osmosis. It requires continual proactive responsiveness to foster an inclusive educational culture. Further, it means that we become cultural vigilantes. Exclusion must be exposed in all its forms; the language we use, the teaching methods we adopt, the curriculum we transmit, the relations we establish within our schools, further education colleges and universities.

Central to our vigilance is the continuing need to guard against the conceptual and practical reduction of inclusion as this decade's version of integration. Integration is inherently assimilationist. It holds firm to a traditional notion of ideal types, both of people and institutions. According to this model the emphasis is upon deficit, diagnosis, categorisation and individual treatment (Barton 1987). The challenge for the integrationist is how to regulate the flow of different students:

- what streams they go into in the regular school;
- what additional resources will be required to contain these defective and difficult students in the regular school (albeit at the margins); or

- what special settings will they occupy outside of regular educational provision.

This is the continuum that integrationists are often reduced to.

Inclusion commences from an entirely different set of assumptions. Allan Luke from the University of Queensland has referred to the need for paradigm busting in education. The integrationists', and for that matter – special educationists' – conceptual tools are inadequate and entirely inappropriate to the task of inclusion, just as the old analytic frames had lost their acuity on a changing map of political economy. As we speak, our language is the talk of cultural change. The project of inclusion is a political and social struggle to enable the valuing of difference and identity. For many education workers inclusion is reduced to a technical problem of people and resource management (Slee 1996).

At the heart of the difference between integration and inclusion lies our next general observation. The traditional special education discourse is one in which the voices of the professions dominate. They speak for people with disabilities and they 'know' them – rendering them the objects for professional work. Within an inclusive education dialogue there is a plurality of voices devoid of existing hierarchies of status and privilege. People themselves are enfranchised to suggest their preferences for a level of participation in education that contributes to improving their quality of life. The organisation of inclusive education presents a stark contrast to the traditional position of professionals who control educational decision-making. Inclusive education proceeds from larger political, as opposed to technical, questions about the nature of society and the status afforded to people in varying forms and structures of social organisation. A political movement in the first instance, inclusion is about establishing access for all people. It is not conditional, nor does it speak about partial inclusion. Its impetus emanates from the recipients of professional services rather than from being orchestrated by professionals themselves.

Following this observation come a particularly perplexing and provocative set of questions about a new order for the role of expertise. Those of us working in the academy may be especially challenged. We have, over a long period of time, become quite comfortable in our traditional knowledge and the status conferred upon us. Access to well-stocked libraries may not give greater insight than may be gained from directly listening to marginalised and excluded people themselves. Inclusive schooling is not secured by having trainee teachers take units in special needs education. The challenge, it seems to us, is how a platform is erected for people of difference in the academy itself. We have witnessed this dedication to including hitherto excluded voices in the field of disability studies where Mike Oliver and Colin Barnes established disabled researchers within research projects about disability.

Inclusive education is a distinctly political, 'in-your-face', activity. As such it may be discomforting, challenging professional expertise and is seen by some to deskill professionalism. The concern is to bring sub-groups in from the margins; it is a reordering of the politics of knowledge. This new politics of education introduces complexity at a time when politicians and bureaucrats are looking for standardisation and simpler sets of quick fixes. It welcomes uncertainty where the political imperative is establishing certainty. Integration and its attendant 'codes of practice' were about technical solutions to technical problems about the fit or misfit of people in stable organisations. Our observation issues a rejection in acknowledging the implicit assumption of a new politics, a new set of speakers in the conversation about inclusive schools for the future. Many people, including some of our readers, become impatient and profoundly frustrated by this. It seems to us that they are looking for solutions before establishing the issues. We await The Fourth Way! Stephen Ball's (1998) urging for the field of education studies to dare to think 'otherwise', eschewing the reductionist imperatives of school effectiveness research, encourages us to trust the force of imagination and risk-taking.

Our next observation comes from our discussion of the work of a colleague, Mel Ainscow. In an interview for a recent research project he talks of inclusive education in the following terms:

> 'Inclusive education is really a process of people inquiring into their own context to see how it can be developed and it is a process of growth. It is a social process and it engages people in making sense of their experience and helping one another to question their experience and their context to see how things can be moved forward.' (Mel Ainscow, interviewed 26 October 1998)

We share this view. In particular, we are encouraged by the acknowledgment that it is a process of growth. After all, if you are really listening to voices from the outside how can old positions remain the same?

Is there a place for comparative studies such as this? The field of comparative education studies was an essentially staid and steadfastly unreflexive area of educational inquiry. There was a tendency to fix countries and people in generalities and then draw comparison between countries, or at least between these general and subjective descriptions, as neat and distinct case studies. Fluidities, movement and hybridity within and between countries were eschewed as they interrupted the neatness of the work. There existed a view of the nation state as an acceptable signifier of the character of the people and systems of education within the defined geographic boundaries. Once again we believe we are dealing with 'messiness' (Ball 1990). Modernist narratives of national boundaries and race are found analytically wanting (Luke and Luke 1998). Recent studies of inclusive education across cultural/national boundaries (Pijl *et al.* 1997, Booth and Ainscow 1998, Daniels and Garner 1999) attest to new complexities in comparative educational research.

Booth and Ainscow (1998, pp. 241–2) recognise the difficulties in taking case studies examples from a range of different countries. They identify a need to warn researchers that they should no longer represent an official view gleaned from government policy documents that often display inconsistencies and problems of conceptualisation as the national view of inclusion and exclusion. Hence our remarks on inclusive education and educational exclusion in Australia and England and Wales in the next section of our conversation are not offered as definitive; they remain observations from our particular vantage positions. Moreover, talking about inclusion cannot be pursued in a policy vacuum. Christie (1999) warns against the generation of further 'context blind' government initiatives relating to curriculum and pedagogy. Inclusive education begins from the context of policy and the recognition of the complexity of identity and difference.

Reflections from where we sit

What follows is an attempt by both of us to tell the other what we are observing from our part of the world at this moment in time. We do not claim definitive overviews of the state of play within our respective countries. Simply, this is a catching up with each other about some of the major issues as they emerge from our organising questions. Jenny commences by reflecting upon inclusive education in England and Wales. We then attempt to make sense of the dialogue by drawing out the major themes.

Question One: How can schools create an inclusive culture in a climate of educational markets and school effectiveness?

Jenny: The current emphasis in schools in England and Wales is upon academic achievement, high standards of behaviour and consistency of curricular approach. Whilst this can be praised as an equality of opportunity model, it reinforces an individualised, competitive attitude which rests uneasily with the emphasis on community values, cooperation and social learning which form integral elements of inclusive education. The high degree of competition between schools has led to patterns of selection such that some schools have disproportionate numbers of high-achieving pupils and others of pupils with learning and behavioural difficulties. There is widespread recognition that we are operating in an education market, where schools compete for customers. Yet, despite the concept of 'value-added', all schools are judged on the same league tables. It is a particular challenge for an inclusive school to demonstrate that it is also an effective school by current government criteria.

Roger: While the mechanisms for raising standards and achieving a climate of effectiveness are vastly different between the two countries, the discourse resonates. We too are entrapped within a compensatory model of distributive justice. Thankfully, Australia does not yet have league tables where schools are held up for public acclaim or vilification. In fact, there is legislation in some states of Australia which prohibits the publication of school results. Nevertheless, there have been recent panics about standards of achievement, particularly with regard to literacy and numeracy. It is difficult to generalise across the states and territories of Australia, but a dominant trend has been towards greater levels of standardisation and the pressure for testing to provide evidence of improvement. All of this places an agenda for inclusive education at the margins of education policy. I say this knowing that many education departments pride themselves on having specific policies pursuant to inclusive education. However, these policies are more concerned with the technical requirements for managing difference in largely unchanged schools. My observations suggest a greater concern for making the existing model of schooling more efficient and effective than for changing school cultures to meet the challenge of valuing the diversity of the student population.

Jenny: Recognising the tensions in trying to create inclusive schools in a climate of effectiveness, I want to give two examples of secondary schools in London which have apparently achieved inclusivity and effectiveness combined. Both schools are located in disadvantaged areas which would now be termed 'social exclusion zones'. They both take high proportions of students with behavioural problems and learning disabilities and both have high percentages of students from a wide range of ethnic minorities. In both examples, the head teachers changed 'failing' schools into effective and popular schools. Among the strategies they used were the following: bringing in black teachers to act as role models; making the school environment attractive and the curriculum relevant to the multicultural community; creating the kinds of support structures which maintained a high ratio of quality, stable staffing; establishing liaison teachers who worked with the local community; addressing issues like racial conflict within the curriculum and community relations. What impressed me about these schools was their close bond with the communities they served and the respect they showed for students and parents. The heads demonstrated their capacity to cope with the market culture and attract sponsorship, so improving their facilities and attracting more potential parents and students. My observations in relation to these examples are: that they have to be inclusive in order to respond to evident needs; they have grown from communities in crisis, to perform an almost healing process; they are probably atypical of secondary schools in England and Wales. Whilst they make excellent case studies of inclusive education, they are about multicultural urban education rather than what is happening in many different parts of the country. If a true comparative study was to be made, they would need to be presented with rural and shire county schools.

Roger: There is much in what you have said, Jenny, that triggers similar impressions of disadvantaged schools in Australia that have managed to achieve authentic forms of inclusion consistent with the imperative of improving the educational outcomes for all of their students. It seems that some schools have the capacity to find spaces in and between education department policy to respond creatively to the needs of their communities. As I reflect upon specific schools I am struck by a sense of their having been determined to change the curriculum, forms of teaching and the culture and structure of their organisations to meet the needs of diverse communities. Inclusion was not restricted to the needs of these so-called 'special needs children', it referred to all comers. I have previously spoken about a school where such a radical process of change led to that school being able to document greater levels of achievement, progress into higher education, vocational training and work than were the surrounding 'academic' schools that held the line and ejected the failing or 'special needs kids' to be admitted by this school to which I refer. Their success with disabled students was equal to their success with Aboriginal students, with students from non-English speaking backgrounds and others who might be seen as students with special needs. I suppose that the point is this: if we are to be effective with the diverse groups of students who come to our schools (rather than those some would like to come to their schools) then a different form of schooling, curriculum and teaching is the base requirement. I'm not sure that the policies to promote school effectiveness in either England and Wales or Australia reflect that yet.

Question Two: Are the concepts of entitlement and inclusion incompatible?

Roger: I would like to think not. All students are entitled to an inclusive education where their various needs are met and they emerge from school to worthwhile destinations with all of the skills and knowledge to enable their full participation in the wider community. That's what I'd like to think. At present in Australia entitlement is a coded reference to a bureaucratic mechanism or set of processes for the distribution of the spoils. It is a resource-linked concept. Entitlement claims, for disabled students, are based upon their capacity to demonstrate their level of individual impairment that results in a reduced capacity to take advantage of the curriculum on offer. A crude accounting is commenced where level of 'ascertained' disability is matched against a schedule of resource provision for that level of disability.

Predictably this mechanism has a number of less than inclusive consequences. People have assumed or been assigned labels connoting defect in order to claim the support they might require to participate in schooling. A form of competition is implicitly encouraged where parents are encouraged to have labels recognised in order that more support is provided. In the areas of learning and attentional disorders there has been a recent upsurge in both the entitlement claims and in the development of new labels and categories. So to summarise, entitlement is a regulatory instrument for allocating scarce resources and this is not about the kind of cultural change in schools that we spoke of earlier.

Jenny: Like you, Roger, I too would like entitlement to be compatible with inclusion. The difficulty seems to arise when there is often fierce competition for limited local government funding and it is those who appear to offer legitimate claims who tend to take priority. The rapid expansion of certain categories in England and Wales, like dyslexia and ADHD, has led to what I would call an 'entitlement imbalance'. We both agree that all learners are entitled to inclusive education but in the present legislative climate of statements and tribunals there are some who are getting a disproportionately large slice of the entitlement cake. The largest and most vulnerable group, those with behavioural and learning difficulties, tend to be least likely to carry this entitlement labelling, which increasingly goes with a medical diagnosis. So they often miss out on precious additional resources.

Roger: It's such an irony that entitlement seems to have moved the focus away from the classroom, away from creating more flexible schools, to the realms of professional diagnosticians and tribunal arbitrators. Incidentally, in Australia we refer to what you call learning difficulties as intellectual disability and it is dyslexia and attentional disorders that come under the general heading of learning disabilities.

Question Three: What does inclusion actually involve?

Roger: New thinking and new practices.

Jenny: I like to present it as metaphor. Whilst integration was the square peg struggling to fit the round holes, inclusion is a circle containing many different shapes and sizes, all interrelating with the whole, and with a caption reading, 'Come in. We celebrate difference here. You can be yourself and not struggle to fit in.' I've recently thought of a three-tier model of inclusion. At the first level, there is surface inclusion, led by policy and notions of school effectiveness. At the second level, there are structural modifications to the school environment and to the curriculum. It is the third level which particularly interests me. This level is that of what I call deep culture, the hidden curriculum of fundamental value systems, rituals and routines, initiations and acceptance which forms the fabric of daily life. It is at this degree of inclusion that real quality of life issues reside. This can be an intangible process whereby students are taught to see themselves as either valued or devalued group members. I feel this depth of inclusion is very hard to monitor or even to fully define but I do believe that it forms the most satisfying type of educational inclusion.

Roger: There are aspects of the hidden curriculum in Australian schools that have been exposed pursuant to more inclusive forms of schooling. I am thinking of the profound contribution of feminist education research and political activism and its deconstruction of patriarchal forms of pedagogical practice, curriculum and school organisational culture. Not that I think the job is complete by any means, and in fact the current 'what about the boys' backlash is an indicator of the work still necessary. Australian education workers and their communities are having to confront racism in ways that they steadfastly refused to do until recently. Celebrations of the National apology to Aboriginal Australians for the enduring impact of European invasion and colonisation has been taken into the curriculum and practices of many schools. Many schools display their 'sorry books' where children, teachers and communities, members can make public their apology. I hasten to add that few people would even think there was a necessity for 'sorry books' to disabled Australians for crimes committed against them. For most educators they are comfortable in their belief that we have been doing good deeds for less fortunate people. Yes, we chip away at the hidden curriculum. But Australia has a journey ahead of it if we are going to shift our thinking to schools and away from notions of defect which are deeply inscribed into the curriculum of traditional schooling.

Question Four: What specific practices help individuals to feel included or excluded?

Jenny: This clearly relates to the nature of the curriculum and teaching methods, school ethos and overall expectations. If there is an emphasis on valuing individual differences rather than on competition, this can help less academic students feel they can contribute. The positive sides of education for active citizenship are inclusive in being collaborative and cooperative. School managers need to take responsibility for fostering a culture of inclusion in the language they use, the topics they select for school assemblies, and in their interactions with staff and students.

Brahm Norwich and I have recently discussed an approach to inclusive education which we termed a 'connective pedagogy' (Corbett and Norwich 1999). In this process the teacher helps individuals to feel included in the curriculum by firstly connecting with them and their learning style and then, secondly, connecting them with the wider community of the classroom, school and local community. Without this first stage, they can remain locationally integrated but not included. Without the second stage, they can have their individual learning needs addressed but be excluded from wider group participation. To achieve this level of connectedness requires a sustained and responsive awareness of the potential barriers to educational inclusion.

Roger: There is convergence between Australia and England and Wales in this domain. In research conducted in the Australian state of Victoria some years ago, we found that rural schools were more likely to be more inclusive than schools in larger urban centres. This can be attributed to two main factors. First, there is no repository of professional expertise outside the school to defer and refer to. Second, the school community started from a clear declaration that these are our children, and whatever problems confront their education, we must sit around the table and find solutions. Hence we observed teachers and teacher aides attending professional development sessions and then teaching the rest of the school that which they had learnt. We also observed close dialogue between the school and its community at all levels.

Where inclusion is seen to be a technical problem for resolution through bureaucratic mechanisms and the deployment of resources and professional expertise, it tends to remain what Jenny has called 'locational integration'. It is a token where students represent what Douglas Biklen (1985) called 'islands in the mainstream'. The extent to which schools in Australia have addressed inclusion as a cultural condition is the extent to which students are actually included. In other words, given that school culture is articulated through curriculum, pedagogy, organisation and ethos, these are the targets for inclusive reform. Certainly resources and professional knowledge are important. However, not all schools in Australia have recognised the centrality of the issues relating to how these are used as a distinguishing factor between assimilation and inclusion.

The Department of Education in Western Australian has attempted to formally acknowledge this careful distinction through its strategies for students at educational risk. The school becomes a target for addressing educational failure and exclusion. There remain tensions within this policy while they simultaneously assert that 20 per cent of the student population is at risk of educational failure. Such target setting, as we know from our reading of the Warnock period, reinforces inclusion as a project of diagnosis and treatment of defective students.

Reflections – global and local themes

A number of themes emerge from this dialogue as overarching key issues for the progress of inclusive education. We will cover three themes in the concluding section of this chapter, but we acknowledge that our discussion is neither exhaustive of the required discussion of the identified themes nor comprehensive in embracing other issues taken up in other chapters in this collection.

Theme One: Paradigm busting

Inclusive education speaks to all students and it assumes a different epistemic stance on a range of issues counter to traditional educational responses to what are typically described as 'problems'. We reject traditional approaches to that which hitherto is referred to as the area of special education or special educational needs. A great deal of theory and practice which forms the special educational tradition is essentially disablist, compounding the patterns of educational and social exclusion we witness in schools and their communities.

Medical models of disability which pivot upon pathological notions of individual defect eschew the deep structure of the 'politics of disablement' (Oliver 1990). Inclusive schooling according to traditional special educational perspectives is seen as a technical problem to be solved through diagnosis and remedial interventions. Typically this generates policies whereby the expert professions are called in to identify the nature and measure the extent of disability. This is followed by highly bureaucratic ascertainment processes where calculations of resources, human and material, are made to support the locating of the disabled child in the regular school or classroom.

Absent from such an approach to 'inclusion' is the acknowledgement that disablement is relational. In other words, schooling itself is more or less disabling or enabling. Inclusive schooling therefore implies that schools too need to be evaluated to determine their impact upon various identities and differences. This view accepts that the technical approach often amounts to little more than variations upon an assimilation score. Inclusion is not assimilation, it speaks to the value and contribution to the patterns within the social mosaic.

Inclusive education embraces a political dialogue against which the educational questions are adjudicated. Just as the argument for the need to liberate education from the grip of patriarchy to improve access and success for girls, and boys, inclusive education accepts that the first step is to challenge the technical and bureaucratically convenient discourses of special educational needs. It needs to be stressed that this does not reflect a 'preoccupation with critique' (Clark *et al.* 1998, p. 162), nor is there an attempt to impose theoretical closure on the field within an inflexible critique of special educational theory and practice. The indivisibility of theory and practice presses us to establish the epistemological foundations of our discourse so that we are not seduced by bureaucratic rearticulations of exclusionary educational cultures. Educational culture is expressed through curriculum, through pedagogy and through the organisational structures and ethos of the institution. It is therefore a fundamental requirement that we test the inclusiveness of these structural elements in moving towards inclusive educational policy. Our purpose is not the refinement of critique (Clark *et al.* 1998, p. 162). Nor are we entrapped in a detached academy. The production of educational practices required for inclusion demand that we 'think otherwise' (Ball 1998) which itself demands disengagement from the investment in traditional special educational culture.

Theme Two: Reconstructing schooling

It has been long argued that inclusive education is not simply a geographical goal. Biklen (1985) wrote of 'islands in the mainstream' to describe the often cited phenomenon of relocating students into the heartland of exclusion. Whether in the same room or safely at a distance, disabled children frequently retain their stranger status in their so called inclusive setting. Inclusive education has a much more profound agenda for educational reform than the placement of children.

Accepting disablement as particular forms of social relations across different institutional contexts, enablement suggests that we consider the social relations of schooling in order to achieve the reconstruction of schooling demanded by inclusive education. And how are the social relations of schooling constituted? They are formed through relations between the pupil and the teacher; between the pupil and what is being taught; between the student and how things are taught. This list goes on. Already we have suggested that curriculum, pedagogy and school organisation are thus capable of being more or less exclusive or inclusive.

The reconstruction of schooling demands different approaches to classroom organisation, to the way teaching occurs, to the development of curriculum content and materials, to assessment and reporting, to the processes of school and community interaction and decision making. Returning to Ainscow (1999, p. 218), he argues that 'inclusive education' is about 'overcoming barriers to participation that may be experienced by any pupils' and that it is not 'concerned only with pupils with disabilities'. In short it is about the culture of schooling for all students. Changing culture warrants interventions in all aspects of its constitution.

Central to the reconstruction of inclusive schooling is the ongoing development of pedagogies of inclusion that recognise individual needs and are receptive to varied learning styles.

Theme Three: Contextualising schooling

As Ballard (1995) contends inclusive schooling will always be unfinished business. Inclusive schooling is signified by the responsiveness of the school to the inevitable and valuable diversity of its community. Educational exclusion is a measure of schools' denial of context. Too often schools teach to an idealised version of the desirable student. Blueprints for the inclusive school are an absurd notion, but as Ainscow (1999) illustrates examples of schools responding to the specific needs of their communities are useful to the greater project of educational reform. The lesson here is in the fundamental importance we attach to the recognition of the specificity of the local context.

This short discussion also amplifies the obstructive capacity of education policy, albeit travelling under the banner of inclusion, to educational inclusion. As Fulcher (1989) has established, policy is made at all levels. Inclusion policy must always be considered with respect to the larger education policy context. Given that the National Curriculum and testing schedules in the UK and moves towards standard curriculum and testing across Australia tend to be context myopic, inclusion needs to issue a challenge to this edifice of education policy. The dramatic increases in exclusions and suspensions (Parsons and Castle 1998) and the establishment of Pupil Referral Units as a legitimate alternative educational provision detract from the imperative of school reform. The marketisation of schools generates greater pupil selectivity on the part of schools and establishes a hierarchy of choosers amongst parents (Gewirtz *et al.* 1995). Students who are not seen to contribute to the performance outcomes of a school, who do not directly advance its League Table performance are regarded with suspicion. The OFSTED denunciations of a range of teaching practices in favour of traditional pedagogical practice also contributes to a policy climate which counters inclusion. Moreover, as we have discussed, many of the policy prescriptions for managing inclusion through Codes of Practice and diagnostic and ascertainment schedules are exclusive in their effect.

Simply put, the project of inclusive schooling requires vigilance at all levels of the education organisation and warrants far-reaching analysis of the articulations between policies across educational sectors. We return to Ballard's (1995) depiction of inclusion as an ideal served through an ongoing project.

A reflection upon form

The manner in which we have chosen to write this chapter may seem both indulgent and exotic. Such impressions may detract from its academic value in the minds of some of our readers. It is our contention that inclusive education proceeds from dialogue. Understanding of local context and the needs of the range of students who enter, or who are blocked from, our schools, may be established through talking. Most importantly this raises the question of voice and the undertaught lesson of listening. We are mindful of a colleague who suggested that the most important lesson for an academic is to know when to stay silent. Who will tell us about student needs? Who is privileged to enter into the conversation? Whose voice carries authority?

Given that this chapter attempts to provide an impression of inclusive education on different sides of the globe, we needed to be listening to each other to appreciate the issues in particular contexts along with their unique and also their overlapping nuances. It seems appropriate that this kind of conversation be supported generally as part of the process of inclusive schooling.

Our conversational format is not only an overt expression of the practice of inclusive education, helping one another to make sense of our experiences and reflections, but it is also a form of assertion. There are many continued sites of hostility and resistance to inclusive education that are found at all levels in the establishment hierarchy. Within the field of inclusive education studies, there are differences and tensions. It is a fragile concept and its parameters are often elusive. For us, this kind of exploratory debate between respected friends is a valuable form of empowerment.

References

Abberley, P. (1987) 'The concept of oppression and the development of a social theory of disability', *Disability, Handicap and Society* **2**(1), 5–19.

Abberley, P. (1992) 'Counting us out: a discussion of the OPCS disability surveys', *Disability, Handicap and Society* **7**(2), 139–55.

Aberdeen City Council Education Department (1996) *Support for Learning Handbook for Professionals*. Aberdeen: Aberdeen City Council.

Agalioti, I. (1992) 'Functional mainstreaming: the evaluation of a program', *Because Difference is a Right*, **44–5**, 21–7.

Ahl, L., Nyberg, E., Persson, B. (1994) *Vad blev det av dom? Specialpedagogisk kompetens i användning*. Specialpedagogisk Bulletin No. 1. Department of Special Education. Göteborg University.

Ainscow, M. (1999) *Understanding the Development of Inclusive Schools*. London: Falmer Press.

Albrecht, G. (1992) *The Disabling Business: Rehabilitation in America*. London: Sage Library of Social Research.

Allan, J. (1996) 'Foucault and special educational needs: a "box of tools" for analysing children's experience of mainstreaming', *Disability and Society* **11**(2).

Allan, J. (1999) *Actively Seeking Inclusion: Pupils with Special Needs in Mainstream Schools*. London: Falmer Press.

Allan, J., Brown, S., Riddell, S. (1995) *Special Educational Needs Provision in Mainstream and Special Schools in Scotland*. Final Report to the Scottish Office. Stirling: University of Stirling.

Anagnostopoulou, E. (1994) 'The integration of pre-school special children in ordinary nurseries', in Kaila, M., Polemikos, N., Filipou, G. (eds) *People with Special Needs*, vol. B, 715–20. Athens: Greek Letters.

Anderson, G. L. (1990) 'Toward a critical constructivist approach to school administration: invisiblity, legitimization, and the study of non-events', *Educational Administration Quarterly* **26**(1), 38–59.

Apple, M. (1995) *Education and Power*. London: Routledge.

Armstrong, F. (1995a) 'Special education in France: passé historic or futur simple?', in O'Hanlon, C. (ed.) *Inclusive Education in Europe*. London: David Fulton Publishers.

Armstrong, F. (1995b) 'Appellation contrôlée ... mixing and sorting in the French education system', in Potts, P., Armstrong, F., Masterton, M. (eds) *Equality and Diversity in Education: National and International Contexts*. London: Routledge.

Armstrong, F. (1995c) 'Comparative perspectives: difference, disability and inclusion: a cross-cultural approach', *Comparative perspectives on special and inclusive education*. Unit 1 in Specialised Module for Diploma/Master of Education, University of Sheffield, Sheffield, UK.

Armstrong, F. (1996) 'Special education in France', in Corbett, A. and Moon, B. (1996) (eds) *Education in France: Continuity and Change in the Mitterand Years, 1981–1995*. London: Routledge.

Armstrong, F. (1998) 'The Curriculum as alchemy: school and the struggle for cultural space', *Curriculum Studies* 6(2), 145–60.

Armstrong, F. (1999) 'Comparative perspectives on difference and difficulty: a cross-cultural approach', in Barton, L. and Armstrong, F. (eds) *Difference and Difficulty: insights, issues and dilemmas*. Sheffield: Department of Educational Studies, University of Sheffield.

Armstrong, F. and Barton, L. (eds) (1999a) *Disability, Human Rights and Education: Cross-cultural Perspectives*. Buckingham: Open University Press.

Armstrong, F., and Barton, L. (1999b) 'Is there anyone there concerned with human rights? Cross-cultural connections, disability and the struggle for change in England', in Armstrong, F. and Barton, L. (eds) *Disability, Human Rights and Education. Cross Cultural Perspectives*. Buckingham: Open University Press.

Baker, J. (1987) *Arguing for Equality*. London: Verso.

Baker, J. and Gaden, G. (1990) *Integration and equality*. Equality Studies Centre, University College, Dublin.

Ball, S. J. (1990) *Politics and Policy Making In Education. Explorations in Policy Sociology*. London: Routledge.

Ball, S. J. (1993) 'Education markets, choice and social class: the market as a class strategy in the UK and the USA', *British Journal of Sociology of Education* 14(1), 3–20.

Ball, S. J. (1994) *Education Reform: A Critical and Post-Structural Approach*. Buckingham: Open University Press.

Ball, S. J. (1998) 'Educational studies, policy entrepreneurship and social theory', in Slee, R., Weiner, G., Tomlinson, S. (eds) *School Effectiveness for Whom?* London: Falmer Press.

Ballard, K. (1995) 'Inclusion, paradigms, power and participation', in Clark, C., Dyson, A., Millward, A. (eds) *Towards Inclusive Schools?* London: David Fulton Publishers.

Ballard, K. (ed.) (1999) *Inclusive Education. International voices on disability and justice* London: Falmer Press.

Bannerman Foster, S. (1987) *The Politics of Caring.* Lewes: Falmer Press.

Bardis, P. (1994) 'The mainstreaming of children with special needs: the content and philosophy of the mainstreaming process', in Kaila, M., Polemikos, N., Filipou, G. (eds) *People with Special Needs*, vol. B, 720–25. Athens: Greek Letters.

Barnes, C. (1990) *'Cabbage Syndrome': The Social Construction of Dependence.* London: Falmer Press.

Barnes, C. (1991) *Disabled People in Britain and Discrimination: A Case for Anti-Discrimination Legislation.* London: Hurst & Co.

Barnes, C. (1992) 'Qualitative research: valuable or irrelevant?' *Disability, Handicap and Society* 7(2), 115–24.

Barnes, C. (1996) 'Theories of disability and the origins of the oppression of disabled people in Western society', in Barton, L. (ed.) *Disability and Society: Emerging Issues and Insights.* Harlow: Addison, Wesley Longman.

Barnes, C., Mercer, G., Shakespeare, T. (1999) *Exploring Disability: A Sociological Introduction.* Oxford: Blackwell Publishers.

Bartlett, W. *et al.* (1994) *Quasi Markets in the Welfare State.* Bristol: SAUS.

Barton, L. (1988) *The Politics of Special Educational Needs.* Lewes: Falmer Press.

Barton, L. (1991) 'Disability: the necessity of a socio-political perspective'. Paper given at International Conference in Oakland, California, 1–27.

Barton, L. (1995) 'Conclusion', *Comparative perspectives on special and inclusive education.* Unit 11 in Specialised Module for Diploma/Master of Education, University of Sheffield, Sheffield, UK.

Barton, L. (1997) 'Inclusive education: romantic, subversive or realistic?', *International Journal of Inclusive Education*, 1(3), 231–42.

Barton, L. (ed.) (1987) *The Politics of Special Educational Needs.* Lewes: Falmer Press.

Barton, L. (ed.) (1996) *Disability and Society: Emerging Issues and Insights.* Harlow: Addison Wesley Longman.

Barton, L. and Oliver, M. (1992) 'Special needs: a personal trouble or public issue?', in Arnot, M. and Barton, L. (ed.) *Voicing Concerns: Sociological Perspectives on Contemporary Education Reforms.* Oxford: Triangle Books.

Barton, L. and Slee, R. (eds) (1999) 'Competition, selection and inclusive education', *International Journal of Inclusive Education* 3(1), (Special issue).

Belmont, B. and Verillon, A. (1997) 'Intégration scolaire d'enfants handicapés à l'école maternelle: partenariat entre enseignants de l'école ordinaire et professionnels spécialés', *Revue Française de Pédagogie* 119.

Belmont, B. and Verillon, A. (1999) 'Integration of disabled children in French schools: partnership between mainstream school teachers and specialist professionals', *European Journal of Special Needs Education* **14**(1), 1–11.

Benn, C. and Chitty, C. (1996) *Thirty years on: is comprehensive education alive and well or struggling to survive?* London: David Fulton Publishers.

Bernstein, B. (1996) *Pedagogy: Symbolic Control and Identity, Theory, Research, Critique.* London: Taylor and Francis.

Biklen, D. (1985) *Achieving the Complete School.* New York: Teachers' College Press.

Binet, A. and Simon, T. (1907) *Les enfants anormaux: Guide pour l'admission en classe de perfectionnement*

Bitzarakis, P. (1989) 'Social racism: people with special needs', *Because Difference is a Right*, **6–7**, 61–2.

Booth, T. (1983) 'Integrating special education', in Booth, T. and Potts, P. (eds) *Integrating Special Education.* Oxford: Blackwell.

Booth, T. (1988) 'Challenging conceptions of integration', in Barton, L. (ed.) *The politics of special educational needs.* London: Falmer Press.

Booth, T. (1995) 'Mapping inclusion and exclusion: concepts for all?', in Clark, C., Dyson, A., Millward, A. (eds) *Towards Inclusive Schools?* London: David Fulton Publishers.

Booth, T. (1996) 'A perspective on inclusion from England', Cambridge Review of Education, *Cambridge Journal of Education* **26**(1), 87–99.

Booth, T. and Ainscow, M. (eds) (1998a) *From Them to Us. An International Study of Inclusion in Education.* London: Routledge.

Booth, T. and Ainscow, M. (1998b) 'USA response: liberating voices?', in Booth, T. and Ainscow, M. (eds) *From them to us. An international study of inclusion in education.* London: Routledge.

Booth, T. and Swann, W. (eds) (1987) *Including Pupils with Disabilities.* Milton Keynes: Open University Press.

Booth, T., Ainscow, M., Dyson, A. (1998) 'Inclusion and exclusion in a competitive system', in Booth, T. and Ainscow, M. (eds) *From them to us. An international study of inclusion in education.* London: Routledge.

Borsay, A. (1997) 'Language and context: issues in the historiography of mental impairments in America, c 1800–1970', *Disability and Society* **12**(1), 137–45.

Bourdieu, P. and Passeron, J. C. (1977) *Reproduction in Education, Society and Culture.* London: Sage.

Bourne, J., Bridges, L., Searle, C. (1994) *Outcast England: How Schools Exclude Black Children.* London: Institute of Race Relations.

Bourneville, D. M. (1906/1907) 'Quelques réflexions à propos des enfants anormaux à Paris', *Revue Philanthropic*, Paris.

Branson, J. and Miller, D. (1989) 'Beyond integration policy – the deconstruction of disability', in Barton, L. (ed.) *Integration: Myth or Reality?* Lewes: Falmer Press.

Brantlinger, E. (1997) 'Using ideology: cases of non-recognition of the politics of research and practice in special education', *Review of Educational Research* **67**(4), 425–59.

Breen, R. (1986) *Subject Availability and Student Performance in the Senior Cycle of Irish Post-Primary Schools.* Dublin: Economic and Social Research Institute.

Breen, R. *et al.* (eds) (1990) *Understanding Contemporary Ireland: State, Class and Development in the Republic of Ireland.* Dublin: Gill and Macmillan.

Campbell, J. and Oliver, M. (1996) *Disability Politics. Understanding Our Past, Changing Our Future.* London: Routledge.

Carr, M. (1988) 'The practice of within class ability grouping: a study of teachers and pupils in the Stranorlar INTO Branch, Co. Donegal', unpublished MEd thesis, University College Dublin.

Christie, P. (1999) 'Inclusive education in South Africa: achieving equity and majority rights', in Daniels, H., Garner, P. (eds) *World Yearbook of Education 1999: Inclusive Education.* London: Kogan Page.

CISP (1998) Consortium on Inclusive Schooling Practices Issue Brief, 'Including Students with Disabilities in Accountability Systems', vol. 3(2).

Clancy, P. (1988) *Who Goes to College?* Dublin: Higher Education Authority.

Clancy, P. (1995) 'Education in the Republic of Ireland: The project of modernity?', in Clancy, P. *et al.* (eds) *Irish Society: Sociological Perspectives.* Dublin: Institute of Public Administration in association with The Sociological Society of Ireland.

Clark, C., Dyson, A., Millward, A. (1998) *Theorising Special Education. Time to Move On?* in Clark, C., Dyson, A., Millward, A. (eds) *Theorising Special Education.* London: Routledge.

Cohen, A. and Hugon, A. (1995) *Nouveaux Lycées, Nouveaux Pédagogiques.* Paris: Harmattan/CRESAS.

Condorcet, (1792) Rapport et projet de décret sur l'organistation de l'instruction publique: Paris.

Conference of Major Religious Superiors (CMRS) (1989) *Inequality in Schooling in Ireland: The Role of Selective Entry and Placement.* Milltown Park, Dublin 6.

Coolahan, J. (ed.) (1994) *Report on the National Education Convention.* Dublin: The National Education Convention Secretariat.

Cooney, T. (1995) 'Recommendations', in Callaghan, P. (ed.) *Legislation, Disability and Higher Education.* Dublin: AHEAD Education Press.

Corbett, J. (1995) *Bad Mouthing: The Language of Special Educational Needs.* London: Taylor and Francis.

Corbett, J. (1997) 'Include/exclude: redefining the boundaries', *International Journal of Inclusive Education* 1(1), 55–64.

Corbett, J. and Norwich, B. (1999) 'Learners with special educational needs', in Mortimore, P. (ed.) *Understanding Pedagogy and its Impact on Learning.* London: Paul Chapman.

Corker, M. (1998) 'Disability discourse in a post-modern world', in Shakespeare, T. (ed.) *The Disability Reader.* London: Cassell.

Courteix, M-C. (1999) 'Les élèves à besoins éducatifs spécifiques: intérêts et limites d'une notion', *Bulletin de liaison de l'adaptation et de l'integration scolaires*, No. 3, January.

Daniels, H. and Garner, P. (eds) (1999) *Inclusive Education.* London: Kogan Page.

Dant, T. and Gregory, S. (1991) 'The Social Construction of Deafness', Unit 8, *Issues in Deafness.* Milton Keynes: Open University Press.

Davazoglou, A. (1994) 'Issues concerning people with special needs in rural areas', in Kaila, M., Polemikos, N., Filipou, G. (eds) *People with Special Needs*, vol. B, 891–95. Athens: Greek Letters.

Davis, L. (1997) ' Constructing normalcy: The bell curve, the novel and the invention of the disabled body', in Davis, L. (ed.) *The Disability Studies Reader.* London: Routledge.

Democrat and Chronicle (1999) 'School standards called too stressful', Rochester, New York, 3 June.

Department for Education (DfE) (1994) *The Code of Practice on the Identification and Assessment of Children with Special Educational Needs.* London: DfE.

DfEE (1997a) *Excellence in Schools.* London: HMSO.

DfEE (1997b) *Excellence for All Children; Meeting Special Educational Needs.* London: DfEE.

DfEE (1998) *Meeting Special Educational Needs: A programme of action.* London: DfEE Publications.

DfEE (1999a) *Special educational needs: consultation document on the proposed revision of the SEN code of practice.* London: DfEE.

DfEE (1999b) *Draft guidance, Social inclusion: pupil support.* London: DfEE.

DfEE (1999c) *Excellence in Cities.* London: DfEE.

Department of Education and Science (DES) (1978) *Special Educational Needs* (The Warnock Report). London: HMSO.

Devine, D. (1991) 'A study of reading ability groups: primary school children's experiences and views', unpublished MEd thesis, University College Dublin.

Digby, A. (1996) 'Contexts and perspectives', in Wright, D. and Digby, A. (eds) *From Idiocy to Mental Deficiency: Historical Perspectives on People with Learning Difficulties.* London: Routledge.

District Document (1998) Inclusion Committee Report, April. Rochester City School District, Rochester, New York.

District Public Relations Document (1995) *Inclusive Schooling Means Belonging*. Lawrence, Kansas: Lawrence Public Schools.

Dockrell, J. and McShane, J. (1993) *Children's Learning Difficulties*. Oxford: Blackwell.

Doyal, L. and Gough, I. (1991) *A Theory of Human Need*. Basingstoke: Macmillan.

Driver, S. and Martell, L. (1997) 'New Labour's communitarianisms', *Critical Social Policy* **52**(17), 27–46.

Drudy, S. and Lynch, K. (1993) *Schools and Society in Ireland*. Dublin: Gill and Macmillan.

Ds. 1994:56 (1994) *Skolans kostnader, effektivitet och resultat – en branschstudie*. Stockholm: Finansdepartementet.

Dunn, L. (1968) 'Special education for the mildly retarded – is much of it justifiable', *Exceptional children* **35**(1), 5–22.

Elliott, J. and Thurlow, M. (1997, March) 'Opening the door to education reform: understanding educational assessment and accountability'. Boston: The Federation for Children with Special Needs.

Englund, T. (1993) 'Education for public or private good', in Swedish Agency for Education (ed.) *Towards Free Choice and Market-Oriented Schools. Problems and Promises*. Report No. 2. Stockholm.

Equality Studies Centre, University College Dublin (1994) 'Equality, Status and Disability'. Paper prepared for the Commission on the Status of People with Disabilities.

Feagin, J. R. (1998) *The new urban paradigm: critical perspectives on the city*. Langham, M.D. Rowman & Littlefield Publishers, Inc.

Ferguson, D. L. (1995) 'The real challenge of inclusion: confessions of a "rabid inclusionist"' *Phi Delta Kappan* **77**(4) 281–7.

Fielding, M. (1999) 'Communities of learners', in O'Hagan, R. (ed.) *Modern Educational Myths*. London: Kogan Page.

Florian, F. (1999) Personal communication.

Forum of People with Disabilities (1993) *Social Welfare Policy Document*. City Arts Centre, 23 Moss Street, Dublin 2.

Foucault, M. (1967) *Madness and Civilization. A History of Insanity in the Age of Reason*. London: Tavistock.

Foucault, M. (1979) *Discipline and Punish: The Birth of the Prison*. Harmondsworth: Penguin Books. (First published as *Surveiller et punir: Naissance de la prison*, 1975.)

Foucault, M. (1982) 'The subject and power', in Dreyfus, H. and Rabinow, P. (eds) *Michel Foucault: Beyond Structuralism and Hermeneutics*. Brighton: Harvester.

Fragou, A. (1989) 'The proposal of A. Fragou', *Because Difference is a Right*, **6–7**, 62–4.

Freire, P. (1985) *The Politics of Education: Culture, Power and Liberation.* London: Macmillan.

Fulcher, G. (1989) *Disabling Policies? A Comparative Approach to Education Policy and Disability.* London: Falmer Press. (Republished 1999 and obtainable from Philip Armstrong Publications, 1 Collegiate Crescent, Sheffield, S10 2BA.)

Fulcher, G. (1993) 'Schools and contests: a reframing of the effective schools debate?', in Slee, R. (ed.) *Is There A Desk With My Name On It? The Politics of Integration.* London: Falmer Press.

G. M. (1983) 'What is the 1143', *Because Difference is a Right,* 1, 32–7.

Gaden, G. (1992) 'Integrated education, mental disability and respect for persons', *Irish Educational Studies* 12.

Galloway, D. and Goodwin, C. (1987) *The Education of Disturbing Children. Pupils with learning and adjustment difficulties.* London: Longman.

Gardner, H. (1985) *Frames of Mind: The Theory of Multiple Intelligences.* London: Paladin.

Gewirtz, S., Ball, S. J., Bowe, R. (1995) *Markets, Choice and Equity in Education.* Buckingham: Open University Press.

Giddens, A. (1986) *Sociology. A Brief but Critical Introduction.* 2nd edn. Basingstoke: Macmillan Education.

Giddens, T. (1999) *The Third Way.* Cambridge: Polity Press.

Goffman, C. (1968) *Asylums,* Harmondsworth: Penguin.

Goodlad, J. I. (1979a). *What Schools Are For.* University of California. Los Angeles.

Griffiths, A. (1999) 'All together now', *Special,* Spring, 20–23.

Hahn, H. (1985) 'Disability policy and the problem of discrimination', *American Behavioral Scientist* **28**(3).

Halstead, J. M. (1988) *Education Justice and Cultural Diversity; an examination of the Honeyford affair, 1984–5,* London: Falmer Press.

Hannan, D. and Boyle, M. (1987) *Schooling Decisions: The Origins and Consequences of Selection and Streaming in Irish Post-Primary Schools.* Dublin: Economic and Social Research Institute.

Hantrais, L. (1996) 'Comparative research methods', in Gilbert, N. (ed.) *Social Research Update 13.* Department of Sociology, University of Surrey.

Happonen, H., Ihatsu, M., Ruoho, K. (1994) Integrering som nödlösning – lyckas det? *Spec-Nytt. Svensk-Finlands Specialpedagogiska förening r.f.* No. 2, 34–8.

Harris, S. (1999) Private communication with Felicity Armstrong, June.

Hart, S. (1996) *Beyond special needs; enhancing children's learning through innovative thinking.* London: Paul Chapman.

Hegarty, S. (1991) 'Toward an agenda for research in special education', *European Journal of Special Needs Education* **6**(2), 87–99.

Hegarty, S. (1993) 'Reviewing the literature on integration', *European Journal of Special Needs Education* **8**(3), 194–200.

Hegarty, S. and Pocklington, K. (1981) *Educating pupils with special needs in ordinary schools*. Windsor: NFER/Nelson.

Heshusius, L. (1982) 'At the heart of the advocacy dilemma: a mechanistic worldview', *Exceptional Children* **49**, 6–13.

Heshusius, L. (1989) 'The Newtonian mechanistic paradigm, special education, and contours of alternatives: an overview', *Journal of Learning Disabilities* **22**(7), 403–15.

Hirschman, A. (1970) *Exit, Voice and Loyalty*. Cambridge, Mass: Harvard University Press.

Hodgkinson, H. (1999, May) 'The New Demographics and its Impact on Urban Schooling'. Address to the State of New York Association of School Superintendents, Rochester, New York.

Looks, B. (1994) *Teaching to Transgress*. New York: Routledge.

Howarth, C. *et al.* (1998) *Monitoring poverty and social exclusion: Labour's inheritance*. York: Joseph Rowntree Foundation.

Hutton, W. (1995) *The State We're In*. London: Jonathan Cape.

Information Bulletin of Special Education (1991) Ministry of National Education, O.E.D.B. Athens: Greece.

Information Bulletin of Special Education (1994) Ministry of National Education, O.E.D.B. Athens: Greece.

Ireland (1992) Department of Education, *Education for a Changing World*, Green Paper on Education. Dublin: The Stationery Office.

Ireland (1993) Department of Education, *Report of the Special Education Review Committee*. Dublin: The Stationery Office.

Ireland (1995) Department of Education, *Charting Our Education Future*, White Paper on Education. Dublin: The Stationery Office.

Ireland (1996) *A Strategy for Equality*. Report of the Commission on the Status of People with Disabilities. Dublin: The Stationery Office.

Ireland (1998) *Education Act*. Dublin: The Stationery Office.

Irish Deaf Society (1993) *Understanding Human Rights of Irish Deaf People*, Second Congress, Trinity College, Dublin, 20 November.

Jonathan, R. (1993) 'Parental rights in schooling', in Munn, P. (ed.) *Parents and Schools: Customers, Managers or Partners?* London: Routledge.

Kassiotakis, M. and Lambrakis, P. A. (1994) 'Greek education and its legislative framework', in Tulasiewicz, W. and Strowbridge, G. (eds) *Education and the Law: International Perspectives*. London: Routledge.

Keefe, L. (1999) 'Examining life in classrooms for students with disabilities and their non-disabled peers'. Paper presented at the Annual Meeting of the American Educational Research Association, Montreal, Canada, April 1999.

Kirk, S., Gallagher, J., Anastasiow, N. (1997) *Special Education*, 8th edn. Boston: Houghton Mifflin.

Kirp, D. (1982) 'Professionalisation as policy choice: British special education in comparative perspective', *World Politics* **XXXIV**(2), 137–74.

Kitsaras, G. (1994) 'The legislative and moral dimension of the education of special children', in Kaila, M., Polemikos, N., Filipou, G. (eds) *People with Special Needs*, vol. A, 87–94. Athens: Greek Letters.

Kivirauma, J. and Kivinen, O. (1988) 'The school system and special education: causes and effects in the 20th century', *Disability, Handicap and Society*, 3(2), 153–66.

Kogidou, D. and Padazis, P. (1994) 'A biographical approach of poverty of people with special needs', in Kaila, M., Polemikos, N., Filipou, G. (eds) *People with Special Needs*, vol. B, 883–90. Athens: Greek Letters.

Kouroublis, P. (1994) 'The role of the statutory legislative interventions in the devitalization of social prejudice', in Kaila, M., Polemikos, N., Filipou, G. (eds) *People with Special Needs*, vol. A, 68–79. Athens: Greek Letters.

Ktenidou, G. (1990) 'A special educational program at the Saint Dimitrious School', *Because Difference is a Right*, **34–5**, 12–15.

Lambropoulou, V. (1994) 'The problems of deaf people in Greece', in Kaila, M., Polemikos, N., Filipou, G. (eds) *People with Special Needs*, vol. A, 464–72. Athens: Greek Letters.

Lane, H. (1993) *The Mask of Benevolence*. New York: Vintage Books.

Lange, C. and Riddell, S. (1999) 'Special educational needs policy and choice: tensions between developments in the US and UK contexts', in McLoughlin, M. and Rouse, M. (eds) *Special Education and Educational Reform in the US and the UK*. London: Routledge.

Language and curriculum access Service (LcaS) (1999) *Enabling progress in multilingual classrooms*. London: London Borough of Enfield.

Lantier, N., Verilon, A., Aublé, J.P., Belmont, B. and Waysand, E. (1994) *Enfants handicapés à l'école: des instituteurs parlent de leurs pratiques*. Paris: INRP-L'Harmattan.

Lgr 62 (1962) *Läroplan för grundskolan. Allmän del.* Stockholm: Skolöverstyrelsen.

Lgr 69 (1969) *Läroplan för grundskolan. Allmän del.* Stockholm: Skolöverstyrelsen.

Lgr 80 (1980) *Läroplan för grundskolan. Allmän del.* Stockholm: Skolöverstyrelsen.

Lipsky, D. K. and Gartner, A. (1997) *Inclusion and School Reform*. Baltimore: Paul H. Brookes Publishing Co.

Logan, K. R. and Keefe, L. B. (1997) 'A comparison of instructional context, teacher behavior, and engaged behavior for students with severe disabilities in general education and self-contained elementary classrooms', *Journal of the Association for Persons with Severe Handicaps* 22(1), 16–27.

Lpo 94 *Läroplaner för det obligatoriska skolväsendet och de frivilliga skolformerna.* Stockholm: Utbildningsdepartementet.

Luke, C. and Luke, A. (1998) 'Theorizing interracial families and hybrid identity: an Australian perspective', unpublished paper from an Australian Research Council funded project.

Lynch, K. (1989) *The Hidden Curriculum: Reproduction in Education: A Reappraisal.* Lewes: Falmer Press.

Marshall, C. (1997) *Feminist Critical Policy Analysis I: A Perspective from Primary and Secondary Schooling.* London: Falmer Press.

Mason, M. (1993) *Inclusion: The Way Forward: A Guide to Integration for Young Disabled Children.* London: Voluntary Organisations Liaison Council for Under Fives.

McCulloch, G. (1994) *Educational Reconstruction: The 1944 Education Act and the Twenty-first Century.* Ilford: Woburn Press.

McDonnell, P. (1992) 'Vested interests in the development of special education in Ireland', *Reach* 5(2), 97–106.

McDonnell, P. and Saunders, H. (1993) 'Sit on your hands: strategies to prevent signing', in Fischer, R. and Lane, H. (eds) *Looking Back: A Reader on the History of Deaf Communities and their Sign Languages.* Hamburg: Signum Press.

Meijer, C. J. W. (1998) *Integration in Europe: Provision for Pupils with Special Educational Needs. Trends in 14 European Countries.* Middelfart: European Agency for Development in Special Needs Education.

Mill, J. S. (1962) *On Liberty.* London: Penguin.

Mittler, P., Brouillette, R., Harris, D. (eds) (1993) *Special Needs Education.* London: Kogan Page.

Morris, J. (1991) *Pride Against Prejudice: A Personal Politics of Disability.* London: Women's Press.

Mousley, J., Rice, M., Tregenza, K. (1993) 'Integration of students with disabilities into regular schools; policy in use', *Disability, Handicap and Society* 8(1), 59–70.

National Association of State Boards of Education (1992, October). *Winners All: A Call for Inclusive Schools.* Alexandria, Va.: Author.

National Commission for Special Needs in Education and Training (NCSNET) (1997) *Quality Education for All, Overcoming Barriers to Learning and Development.* Report of the National Commission for Special Needs in Education and Training. Cape Town: NCSNET, NCESS.

New Mexico Department of Education, Administrative Policy (1991) New Mexico Department of Education, Santa Fe, New Mexico.

Nicodemos, (1994) 'Special education in Greece today', in the Information Bulletin of Special Education, Directorate of Special Education, O.E.D.B, Athens, Greece.

Ny skolstart för Sverige: Nu ska kunskapen fram (1991) *Lärarnas Tidning.* No. 25, 4.

O'Hanlon, C. (1995) 'Inclusive education in Spain and Greece', in Potts, P., Armstrong, F., Masteron, M. (eds) *Equality and Diversity in Education: National and International Contexts*. London: Routledge.

OECD (1995) *Integrating students with special needs into mainstream schools*. Paris: OECD.

Oliver, M. (1989) 'Conductive education: if it wasn't so sad it would be funny', *Disability, Handicap and Society* 4(2), 197–200.

Oliver, M. (1990) *The Politics of Disablement*. London: Macmillan.

Oliver, M. (1992) 'Changing the social relations of research production?' *Disability, Handicap and Society* 7(2), 101–14.

Oliver, M. (1996) 'A sociology of disability or a disablist sociology', in Barton, L. (ed.) *Disability and Society: Emerging Issues and Insights*. Harlow: Addison, Wesley Longman.

Oliver, M. and Barnes, C. (1998) *Disabled People and Social Policy: From Exclusion to Inclusion*. London: Longman.

Papadopoulos, S. (1988) 'The special and therapeutic education in Greece: suggestions for its improvement', *Open School* 20, 19–23.

Papagalia-Katriou, A. (1987) 'The role of parents of children with special needs on the sensitization of the social community', *Because Difference is a Right*, 21–2, 14–9.

Papaioannou, P. (1992) 'The special primary school of Veria. Environmental education: an attempt towards educational and social integration', *Because Difference is a Right*, 44–5, 29–36.

Papaioannou, S. (1984) 'The Social Dimension of Mental Disability: Sensitization and Activation'. Paper presented on 21 November 84 at the 'Three-day Meeting for the Mentally Disabled Child', Athens, Greece.

Parsons, C. and Castle, F. (1998) 'The cost of social exclusion in England', *International Journal of Inclusive Education* 2(4), 277–94.

Paugam, S. (ed.) (1996) *L'exclusion: l'état des savoirs*. Paris: Éditions la découverte.

Persson, B. (1994) 'Aspects of Special Education – Organization, Quality and Outcome'. Paper presented at International Days on Down's Syndrome, Pordenone, Italy, May. Department of Special Education, Göteborg University.

Persson, B. (1995) *Specialpedagogiskt arbete i grundskolan – En studie av förutsättningar, genomförande och verksamhetsinriktning*. Specialpedagogiska rapporter 1995:4. Department of Special Education, Göteborg University.

Persson, B. (1998) *Specialundervisning och differentiering. En studie av grundskolans användning av specialpedagogiska resurser*. Specialpedagogiska rapporter 1995:10. Department of Special Education, Göteborg University.

Philip, M. (1995) 'Michel Foucault', in Skinner, Q. (ed.) *The return of grand theory in the human sciences.* Cambridge, England: Cambridge University Press.

Pijl, J.S., Meijer, C. J., Hegarty, S. (1997) *Inclusive Education: A Global Agenda.* London: Routledge.

Plaisance, E. (1996) 'Les enfants handicapés à l'école', in Paugam, S. (ed.) (1996) *L'exclusion: l'état des savoirs.* Paris: Éditions la découverte.

Poplin, M. and Stone S. (1992) 'Paradigm shifts in instructional strategies: from reductionism to holistic/constructivism', in Stainback, W. and Stainback, S. (eds) *Controversial Issues Confronting Special Education.* Boston: Allyn and Bacon.

Potts, P. (1983) 'Medicine, morals and mental deficiency', *Oxford Review of Education* **9**(3), 181–96.

Potts, P., Armstrong, F. and Masterson, M. (eds) (1995) *Equality and Diversity in Education 2: National and International Cotext.* London: Routledge.

Power, A. and Mumford, K. (1999) *The slow death of great cities? Urban abandonment or urban renaissance.* York: York Publishing Services.

Prop. 1988/89:4. (1988) *Regeringens proposition om skolans utveckling och styrning.* Stockholm: Utbildningsdepartementet.

Radford, J. (1994) 'Intellectual disability and the heritage of modernity', in Rioux, M. and Bach, M. (eds) *Disability is not Measles.* Ontario: Roeher Institute.

Riksförbundet FUB (1994) *Projekt om utvecklingsstörning vid kommuner, landsting och forskningsenheter.* FUB Box 55615, S-102 14 Stockholm, Sweden.

Rioux, M. and Bach, M. (eds) (1994) *Disability is not Measles: New Research Paradigms in Disability.* Ontario: Roeher Institute.

Roach, V. and Raber, S. (1997) 'State educational reforms: District response and the implications for special education. A cross-site analysis based on four case studies'. Alexandria, Va.: Center for Policy Research on the Impact of General and Special Education Reform, National Association of State Boards of Education.

Robitaille, D. and Garden, R. (1989). *The IEA Study of Mathematics II; Contexts and Outcomes of School Mathematics. Oxford:* Pergamon

Rosenqvist, J. (1993) 'Special education in Sweden', *European Journal of Special Needs Education* **8**(1), 59–73.

Rosenqvist, J. (1994) *Specialpedagogiska forskningsmiljöer – En analyserande översikt.* Department of Education, Göteborg University.

Ryan, J. and Thomas, F. (1980) *The Politics of Mental Handicap.* Harmondsworth: Penguin.

Salpistis, S. (1987) 'Becoming a parent of a mentally or physically disabled child', *Because Difference is a Right,* **21–2**, 49–53.

Sarason, S. B. and Doris, J. (1982) 'Public policy and the handicapped: the case of mainstreaming', in Lieberman, A. and McLaughlin, M. (eds) *Eighty-first Yearbook of the National Society for the Study of Education.* Chicago: NSSE.

Saunders, H. (1997) 'Growing up deaf in Ireland', unpublished thesis, M. Phil. in Applied Linguistics, University of Dublin, Trinity College.

Schnorr, R. (1990) 'Peter? He comes and goes ... "First graders"' perspective on a part-time mainstream student', *Journal of the Association for Persons with Severe Handicaps* **15**(4), 231–40.

Scottish Education Department (SED) (1978) *The Education of Pupils with Learning Difficulties in Primary and Secondary Schools in Scotland.* Edinburgh: HMSO.

Scottish Office (1991, updated 1995) *The Parents' Charter in Scotland.* Edinburgh: The Scottish Office.

Scottish Office Education Department (SOED) (1993) *A Parents' Guide to Special Educational Needs.* Edinburgh: The Scottish Office.

Scottish Office Education Department (SOED) (1994) *Effective Provision for Special Educational Needs. A Report by HM Inspectors of Schools.* Edinburgh: The Scottish Office.

Scottish Office Education and Industry Department (SOEID) (1998) *Special Educational Needs in Scotland: A Discussion Paper.* Edinburgh: HMSO.

Scull, A. T. (1979) *Museums of Madness: The Social Organization of Insanity in Nineteenth-Century England.* London: Penguin Books.

Sebba, J. (1997) *What works in inclusive education?* Ilford: Barnardos.

Sebba, J. and Ainscow, M. (1996) 'International developments in inclusive education – mapping the issues', *Cambridge Journal of Education* **26**, 5–19.

Shakespeare, T., Atkinson, D., French, S. (eds) (1993) *Reflecting on Research Practice: Issues in Health and Social Welfare.* Buckingham: Open University Press.

Shapiro, M. J. (1981) 'Disability and the politics of constitutive rules', in Albrecht, G. L. (ed.) *Cross-National Rehabilitation Policies*, 84-96. California: Sage Publications.

Shaw, L. (1990) *Each Belongs: Integrated Education in Canada.* London: Centre for Studies on Integration in Education.

Sibley, D. (1995) *Geographies of Exclusion.* London: Routledge.

Simon, B. (1991) *Education and the social order 1940–1990.* London: Lawrence and Wishart.

Skr. 1993/94:183. *Regeringens skrivelse 1993/94:183. Utvecklingsplan för skolväsendet.* Stockholm.

Slee, R. (1995) 'Inclusive education: from policy to school implementation', in Clark, C., Dyson A., Millward, A. (eds) *Towards Inclusive Schooling: A New Agenda for Special Needs?*, 30–53. New York: Teachers' College Press.

Slee, R. (1996) 'Inclusive Education in Australia? Not Yet?', *Cambridge Journal of Education* **26(1)**, 19–32.

Slee, R. (ed.) (1993) *Is There A Desk With My Name On It? The Politics of Integration*. London: Falmer Press.

Social Exclusion Unit (1998) *National strategy for neighbourhood renewal*. London: The Cabinet Office.

Söder, M. (1984) *Anstalter för utvecklingsstörda – En historisk-sociologisk beskrivning av utvecklingen*. Stockholm: Ala.

SOU 1961:30. *Grundskolan. 1957 års skolberedning*. Stockholm: Ecklesiastikdepartementet.

Spelman, B. and Griffin, S. (eds) (1994) *Special Educational Needs – Issues for the White Paper*. Proceedings of a cooperative theme conference in response to the Report of the Special Education Review Committee, University College Dublin, 21–22 January.

Stalker, K. (1995) 'The antinomies of choice in community care', in Baldwin, S. and Barton, P. (eds) *The International Handbook of Community Care*. London: Routledge.

Stasinos, D. (1991) *Special Education in Greece: Concepts, Policies and Practices. State and Private Initiatives*. Athens: Gutenberg, Greece.

Stiker, H-J. (1996) 'Handicap et exclusion. La construction sociale du handicap', in Paugam, S. (ed.) (1996) *L'exclusion: l'état des savoirs*. Paris: Éditions la découverte.

Stirling, M. (1992) 'How many pupils are being excluded?' *British Journal of Special Education* **19(4)**, 128–30.

Stukát, K-G. and Bladini, U-B. (1986) *Svensk specialundervisning. Intentioner och realiteter i ett utvecklingsperspektiv*. Rapport. Department of Education, Göteborg University.

Swain, J. *et al.* (eds) (1993) *Disabling Barriers – Enabling Environments*. London: Sage in association with the Open University.

Taylor, G. and Laurenzi, C. (1991) 'Deaf people in hearing worlds: the manufacture of disadvantage', Unit 6, *Issues in Deafness*. Milton Keynes: Open University Press.

Teacher Training Agency (1998a) *National standards for special educational needs co-ordinators*. London: TTA.

Teacher Training Agency (1998b) *National standards for special educational needs (SEN) specialist teachers (consultation)*. London: TTA.

The Combat Poverty Agency, the Forum of People with Disabilities and the National Rehabilitation Board (1994) 'Disability, Exclusion and Poverty'. Papers from a National Conference, The Combat Poverty Agency, 8 Charlemont Street, Dublin 2.

Thrupp, M. (1999) *Schools Making a Difference. Let's Be Realistic!* Buckingham: Open University Press.

Tomlinson, J. (1997) 'Inclusive learning: the report of the committee of inquiry into the post-school education of those with learning difficulties and/or disabilities in England, 1996', *European Journal of Special Needs Education* **12**(3), 184–96.

Tomlinson, S. (1982) *A Sociology of Special Education*. London: Routledge and Kegan Paul.

Towler, M. A. (1998) 'Failing our children: the class of 97', in *City Newspaper*, 9–15 December, 5–10, Rochester, New York.

Tsiakalos, G. (1989) 'The proposal of George Tsiakalou', *Because Difference is a Right*, **6–7**, 64–8.

Tutt, N. (1985) 'The unintended consequences of integration', *Educational and Child Psychology* **2**(3), 30–138.

UNESCO (1998) *From special needs education to education for all: a discussion paper*. Paris: UNESCO.

US Department of Education (1994) Sixteenth Annual Report to Congress on the implementation of the Individuals with Disabilities Education Act. Washington, DC: Author.

US Department of Education (1997) Nineteenth Annual Report to Congress on the implementation of the Individuals with Disabilities Education Act. Washington, DC: Author.

US Department of Education (1999) Twentieth Annual Report to Congress on the implementation of the Individuals with Disabilities Education Act. Washington, DC: Author.

US EDInfo listserve (1999), Friday, 12 March, 'Final IDEA Regulations and Report on Implementation of IDEA'.

Vial, M. (1990) *Les enfants anormaux à l'école. Aux origines de l'éducation spécialisée 1882–1909*. Paris: Armand Colin.

Vlachou, A. (1997) *Struggles for Inclusive Education: An Ethnographic Study*. London: Open University Press.

Vlachou, A. and Barton, L. (1994) 'Inclusive education: teachers and the changing culture of schooling', *British Journal of Special Education* **21**(3), 105–107.

Vlachou-Balafoutis, A. (in press) 'Equality and full participation for all? School practices and special education/integration', in Armstrong, F. and Barton, L. (eds) *Disability, Human Rights and Education. Cross Cultural Perspectives*. London: Open University Press.

Wang, M. C., Reynolds, M. C., Walberg, H. J. (1995) *Handbook of Special and Remedial Education: Research and Practice*, 2nd edn. Oxford: Elsevier Science.

Ware, L. (1994) 'Innovative instructional practices: a naturalistic study of the structural and cultural conditions of change', unpublished doctoral dissertation, University of Kansas.

Ware, L. (1995a) 'The aftermath of the articulate debate: the invention of inclusive education', in Clark, C., Dyson, A., Millward, A. (eds.) *Towards Inclusive Schooling: A New Agenda for Special Needs?*, 127–46. New York: Teachers' College Press.

Ware, L. (1995b) 'Reconstructing welfare policy: voice and empowerment in evaluation research'. Paper presented at Evaluation '95: An International Evaluation Conference co-sponsored by the Canadian Evaluation Society and the American Evaluation Society, Vancouver, British Columbia, November 1995.

Ware, L. (1996a) 'It's not just teaching anymore: school-linked service integration'. Paper presented at the Annual Meeting of the American Educational Research Association, New York, April 1996.

Ware, L. (1996b) 'Defining social justice in the instance of inclusion: critical curriculum in context'. Paper presented at the Annual Meeting of the American Educational Research Association, New York, April 1996.

Ware, L. (1997a) *A cross-case analysis of school-linked services: Critical players in dialogue.* Final research report to the University Affiliated Program. Field initiated research Grant No. HO23D40024 US Department of Education Office of Special Education and Rehabilitative Services.

Ware, L. (1997b) 'Teachers tell: a close analysis of school-linked service integration'. Paper presented at the Annual Meeting of the American Educational Research Association, Chicago, March.

Ware, L. (1997c) 'Secrets and lies: early fieldwork dilemmas'. Paper presented for the Graduate Seminar on Measurement and Research Methodology, sponsored by Division D at the Annual Meeting of the American Educational Research Association, Chicago, March.

Ware, L. (1997d) 'Essays in refusal: accounts of adolescents in special education'. Paper presented at the New Mexico Quarterly Meeting of State Directors of Special Education, Albuquerque, October.

Ware, L. (1998a) 'Sometimes I wonder if we're fooling ourselves', in Booth, T. and Ainscow, M. (eds) *From them to us: An international study of inclusion in education.* London: Routledge.

Ware, L. (1998b) 'Youth with disabilities: voices informing the theoretical discourse on inclusion'. Paper presented at the Annual Meeting of the American Educational Research Association, San Diego, April.

Ware, L. (1999a) 'My kid and kids kinda like him', in Ballard, K. (ed.) *Voices from the Inside: An International Dialogue on Inclusion,* 43–66. London: Falmer Press.

Ware, L. (1999b) 'Inclusive Education', in Gabbard, D. A. (ed.) *Education in the Global Economy: Politics and the Rhetoric of School Reform,* 111–20. New Jersey: Lawrence Erlbaum Publishers.

Ware, L. (1999c) 'Satisfied or sacrificed: claiming ideology in Public Schools'. Paper presented at the International Research Colloquium on Inclusive Education, University of Rochester, New York, 14–17 June 1999.

Ware, L. (1999d) *Teachers Reckoning and Resistance to Inclusion: A Final Report to the New Mexico State Board of Education.* University of New Mexico: Department of Special Education.

Ware, L. and Howarth, S. (1998) 'Tapping the source: pre-service teachers learning from parents'. Paper presented at the Annual ARC New Mexico/SUN TASH, Albuquerque, 23 April.

Whitehead, S. (1992) 'The social origins of normalisation', in Brown, H. and Smith, H. (eds) *Normalisation: A Reader for the Nineties.* London: Tavistock/Routledge.

World Education Report (1993). Paris: UNESCO Publishing.

Xeromeriti, A. (1994) 'Special education: the next 15 years', in Kaila, M., Polemikos, N., Filipou, G. (eds) *People with Special Needs*, vol. B, 616–17. Athens: Greek Letters.

Young, I. (1990) *Justice and the Politics of Difference.* Princeton, NJ: Princeton University Press.

Zoniou-Sideris, A. (1991) *The Disabled and Their Education.* Athens: Vivliogonia.

Zoniou-Sideris, A. (1993) 'The integration of disabled children at the pre-school and school education', *Educational Community* **21**, 21–5.

Zoniou-Sideris, A. (1996) 'Educational policy and the integration of disabled children in ordinary education: speculations, prerequisites, perspectives'. Paper presented at the Second Conference of Special Education, Ionios University.

Index

Lightning Source UK Ltd.
Milton Keynes UK

176435UK00003B/5/A